W9-BZB-368

Landlording As a Second Income

Landlording As a Second Income

The Survival Handbook

Lawrence London, J.D.

MADISON BOOKS

Lanham • New York • Oxford

Copyright © 1994 by Lawrence London

All rights reserved.
No part of this book may be reproduced in any form
or by any electronic or mechanical means, including
information storage and retrieval systems, without written
permission from the publisher, except by a reviewer who
may quote passages in a review.

Published by Madison Books
4720 Boston Way
Lanham, Maryland 20706

12 Hid's Copse Road
Cumnor Hill, Oxford OX2 9JJ, England

Distributed by National Book Network

Previous edition published by Scarborough House

Library of Congress Cataloging-in-Publication Data

London, Lawrence
    Landlording as a second income : the survival handbook /
Lawrence London.
       p.   cm.
    Originally published: Lanham, Md. : Scarborough House, c1994.
    Includes index.
    ISBN 1-56833-109-6 (pbk : alk. paper)
    1. Real estate investment—Handbooks, manuals, etc. 2. Rental
housing—Handbooks, manuals, etc. 3. Landlord and tenant—
Handbooks, manuals, etc. I. Title.
HD1382.5L63   1998
333.33'85'068—dc21   98-11156

ISBN 1-56833-109-6 (pbk : alk. paper)

♾™ The paper used in this publication meets the minimum requirements of
American National Standard for Information Sciences—Permanence of
Paper for Printed Library Materials, ANSI Z39.48–1984.
Manufactured in the United States of America.

CONTENTS

INTRODUCTION

There are hundreds of books on the market on how to make money investing in real estate. Their authors boast of buying property with No Money Down. Authors brag with evangelical glee of buying distressed property and selling a short time later at great profit. All with Other People's Money. Promoters give expensive seminars, and, while hordes of people attend, you wonder how many actually succeed. Do these well-groomed instructors make more money off books and roadshows than through real estate activities?

I also have read No-Money-Down books and have attended Get-Rich-Quick-by-Real-Estate lectures. The oratory flowed; the numbers were dazzling; the cuff-linked dream-merchants were slick. They never had problems with tenants, because they never had any. They bought property for no money down, subdivided it, renovated it, and immediately found buyers—and, of course, always at a tremendous return. For the same reason, they never had financing or management headaches. They always bought cheap and sold dear. I don't doubt these wheeler-dealers, but I never had their luck.

What I missed most was a good book on the do's and don'ts of property management—honest landlording, although I recognize that there is no such word as "landlording." (The closest word the dictionary recognizes is "landlordism" which is defined as the principles and practices of landlords collectively.)

Over the years, I have tried to keep good notes and company with the best real estate managers in the industry. This book encompasses their experience and advice. Through this book I hope to share good landlording techniques with you and spare you from the many pitfalls that befall new landlords. Landlording is an ideal second source of income. It might as well be fun and profitable!

Lawrence London

CHAPTER 1

GETTING STARTED

What's the most profitable real estate?

That was my first question too. A friend referred me to a book high-lighting the careers of twenty-two successful realty moguls. One made a fortune *never* incurring debt while another used Other People's Money. One bought residential housing while another handled commercial property. One rented low-income units while another rented luxury dwellings. One achieved wealth "flipping" contracts while another's policy was never to sell. They *all* succeeded.

If the book had a moral, it was *there is no single way to make money.* Every way can work for you.

Is landlording for you?

Ideally, landlording is a labor of love. You love people, you love real estate, you love tinkering, and you can tolerate bookkeeping and paperwork. If you can answer yes to at least three of these four prerequisites, landlording is for you.

Who has time?

Without doubt, landlording is a second job. What keeps most people from becoming landlords is the amount of time a second job is perceived to take.

How do you make time for landlording? You don't. It just happens. It's Parkinson's Law: Work expands so as to fill the time available for completion.

Let's use bill paying as an example. It's amazing how many people run around town paying bills in person. Some do it because they lack checking accounts, others because they have always done it that way.

When you're a landlord, time is more valuable. Prior habits will have to change. There is no reason to pay bills in person when a postage stamp can do. Don't worry about having to streamline your life to accommodate your new second job. Necessity will do it automatically.

Developing a plan

No storekeeper opens a business without stocking supplies and setting prices and policy. Landlording is no different.

Your real estate plan must go beyond just acquiring property. Strategy includes:
— financing
— tenant selection
— insurance
— rent collection
— repairs
— zoning
— selling (your sales plan begins immediately after acquiring the property).

How do you get started?

In one word: *Deadlines*. You can spend half your life debating whether to become a landlord and the other half looking at various investment properties. For every reason to get into landlording, a case can be made not to. For every reason to buy a certain property, a case can be made to pass.

I was lucky—my first partner liked to jump into a project while I preferred pondering over each facet of a deal. My partner set a deadline: "Larry, 5 p.m. Friday, in or out?" I've been setting deadlines ever since.

No one advocates blindly jumping into deals, but reality says you will go nowhere without deadlines: a deadline for deciding to enter landlording, a deadline to secure financing, a deadline to buy property, etc.

Must you be personally involved with your property?

Realistically, you will find yourself accepting certain responsibilities and delegating others. *You* don't have to fix other people's toilets after a hard day's work. Hired help may be more competent. Indeed, you can turn your entire property administration over to a professional management company. Delegated jobs obviously cut into profit. You must decide early on what jobs you will accept.

Do you need a management company?
Management companies accept responsibility for tenant selection, rent collection, repairs, bookkeeping, etc. Management companies are in a sense your "partners." Some perform well; others do not.

> *Note*: If using a management company, make sure it is *bonded*. Since they collect rents and hold security deposits, you want a bonded company that keeps receipts in a separate account and a company that carries workman's compensation insurance for its employees.

> *Reality*: Some management companies furnish *fidelity bonds* listing the owner as the insured, but at the *owner's* expense. This item is negotiable. Management companies will also require *your* property liability insurance to cover *them*. This too is negotiable.

Management fees are generally 10 percent of rents; again, this is negotiable. Companies may charge a month's rent to screen and secure tenants. They may charge a fixed fee or percent to collect water payments and other charges. Some companies insist on holding tenants' security deposits—again, this item is negotiable.

Some companies charge special *pro-rata* assessments for legal opinions affecting all managed properties; other companies absorb legal and other fees in their operating overhead. These items are all negotiable.

Repairs by management companies
Companies secure the right to perform emergency repairs. They set a dollar amount above which special permission is required, i.e., work over $100.

Some companies charge fixed fees for repairs, especially where their workmen perform repairs.

> *Example*: $40 to unclog a drain; $30 to change a lock, etc.
> Others add a specific percent for overseeing subcontractor's repairs.

Example: If repairs cost $50, the company charges $50, plus 10 percent.

Other companies charge landlords the actual repair cost but expect subcontractors to rebate (some say, *kickback*) a portion of the repair costs to the management company.

Which way is better? There is no correct answer. But, as a landlord, you must know what repairs cost and not be afraid to question unreasonable repair bills.

Advantages to using a management company
—Companies assure that your operations comply with industry-wide standards and applicable laws.
—Companies can sometimes screen tenants better than landlords. They know what questions to ask prospective tenants and have the resources to verify responses. Companies can be impartial.
—Companies can handle day calls and appointments when landlords are at work and have special emergency numbers for off-hours problems.
—Companies have developed lists of competent subcontractors. There are many crooks and incompetents in the repair/improvement business.
—Companies are equipped to handle tenants who don't pay rent. New landlords have to research eviction procedures which can be complicated and sometimes ugly.
—Companies handle many routine bookkeeping chores. Instead of issuing many monthly checks to various service people, you have to issue only one check-to the company. In reality, you do not even do that; the management company does it for you, i.e., the check they give *you* from the tenants' rent has fees and charges already deducted.
—Companies are up-to-date on the law. They know when and how to file for water adjustments. They know whom to contact for tax appeals. They know the various building inspectors and housing codes.
—Companies are excellent referral sources for purchasing additional property, i.e., management companies are first to know when clients want to sell. Hefty commissions can be saved.

Disadvantages to using a management company

—While management companies collect rent on the first of the month, net proceeds are not usually mailed out until the 20th of the month. If you are using rent money to pay current bills, you are almost a month behind.

—Vacancies may take longer to fill. Management companies manage hundreds and sometimes thousands of units, and during the course of a month there are many vacancies. Your vacancy is only one of many that needs to be filled. Often, your vacancy is not even separately advertised but is grouped under a generic heading, i.e., "Apartments/Houses, contact Smith Management Co."

—There is no personal touch. Management companies can't answer specific questions. All they know about the rental is what is on the card.

—In some areas, tenants have to make a separate trip to the management company office. They probably will be charged a non-refundable $15 to $25 application fee for a dwelling they may or may not like. Some management companies, especially on low-income rentals, just hand tenants keys. While they take a "key deposit," there is no negotiation or soothing "sales pitch" at the rental site; it is basically "take it or leave it."

—Since management companies earn extra commission securing tenants, companies may be lax in renting to transient or less than credit-worthy tenants.

—Tenants may be slower on rent payments where a company is involved or may show less respect to company-managed property.

—Tenants who might hesitate to call a landlord with petty problems think nothing of calling a company. Repair costs can sky- rocket.

—Owners are never really sure if what they paid for was actually performed, i.e., a whole roof job, when only patching was done.

—Management companies try to impress landlords with their frugality. They may skimp on repairs or perform repairs in a less than workman-like manner. They often fail to follow through and check whether work was done properly. You may ultimately pay more for repairs that have to be redone.

Other considerations

In choosing a management company, make sure it manages property exclusively. Too often new landlords use as a management company the realtor who sold the property. Some realtors may indeed be good property managers, but it is one thing to run a real estate office and another to be familiar with the ins and outs of property management. *The two are not synonymous.*

Make sure the management company's philosophy matches your own and that the company knows your goals. Some landlords want first-class property management, and some landlords want only minimal maintenance. If your primary goal is to hold property for income, and secondarily for appreciation, you don't want a company pushing you to make major property improvements.

Conversely, if your goal is property appreciation, you want a company sensitive to appreciation potential. Lastly, even if you use a management company, you must still stay involved.

Do you need a lawyer?

Advice books, and of course lawyers, will say, absolutely yes. There are plenty of horror stories out there. Indeed, lawyers can help you avoid hundreds of pitfalls. Laws change daily, and these professionals are experienced and up-to-date.

In reality, the average middle class person does not have a lawyer. It is therefore presumptuous to caution you throughout this book to constantly "check with your lawyer" when the average middle class person has none.

You can still function pretty well without a lawyer. There are knowledgeable bankers, insurance and real estate agents, and other landlords who are similarly up- to-date, and their advice is free. There is a wealth of published material on just about every legal and tax aspect of real estate. And of course, everyone has a brother-in-law, friend, or neighbor "in the business."

Yes, there are risks operating without a paid lawyer at your side, but these are risks that by necessity the average person has chosen to accept. While I have tried to weed out wimpy "check with your lawyer" disclaimers, I apologize in advance for any legal caveats that remain.

> *Note*: For new landlords who want to keep costs down, a cross between a retained lawyer and not having one is membership in a *pre-paid legal plan*. Expect to pay $100 or so a year to have your basic questions answered. Try not to abuse the plan.

Should you establish separate bank accounts?

Definitely yes, even if you plan to have only one or two properties. It is good business to separate rental expenses and income from your personal accounts. The IRS also likes to see that funds are not commingled. For tenants' security deposits, it is *against the law* in most jurisdictions to commingle tenants' funds with your own.

But there are other reasons to open as many separate accounts as you can.

For tenants' security deposits, besides conforming with the law, it is a lot easier to return a security deposit when it doesn't have to come from your personal pocket. Moreover, if the tenant leaves owing money, it is nice to be able to partially repay yourself with the security deposit.

The same is true for all other expenses. As you accumulate property you will have to come up with large sums of money at various times of the year for taxes, insurance, utilities, scheduled repairs, etc. Unless money is tightly squirrelled away, the money will not be available. The point is so obvious, but overlooked by so many.

If you are going to be a landlord, you must place your hand on a stack of rent books and take the following pledge of discipline:

I ____, *hereby pledge to establish separate accounts for security deposits, taxes, utilities, and insurance. I will use these funds only for their earmarked purpose.*

Loyalty to this pledge is for your own financial survival!

Note: If you don't already have a checking account that returns canceled checks, get one. As landlord, you will be writing checks to all sorts of people. Sometimes canceled checks are your only proof that money has been paid. Canceled checks are also valuable at audits.

Should you incorporate?

No, if your game-plan is to own only a dwelling or two. With only a dwelling or two, your liability exposure is less, especially where your properties are heavily mortgaged. Moreover, there are other ways besides incorporation to protect your interests. For instance, happily married couples may consider *not* keeping their investment property in joint names:

Example: John and Mary Jones's personal residence and their invest-ment property are both titled in their joint names as tenants by the entirety. If a tenant obtains a $1,000,000 judgment (over and above their insurance), their investment property *and* their personal resi-dence may be at risk.

Had the Jones' kept their personal residence in their joint names and the investment property in only one of their names, a judgment against the investment property might not necessarily threaten their jointly-held property.

For this same reason, lawyers and insurance agents often advise mar-ried couples to keep their personal residence titled jointly, but to keep cars in individual names. If the individual owner is sued, i.e., John is involved in an accident, it is harder for a plaintiff to go against John's and Mary's jointly-held property. Note, however, that spousal immuni-ty disappears with death of a spouse or divorce.

Keeping it corporate

Placing a property in a corporate name means just that. John and Mary do not own the property; Jones Realty, Inc. owns the property. Incorporation involves both legal and accounting considerations.

Advantages to incorporating

Privacy. Your personal name does not appear in newspapers and public records. This is no small matter. Often, daily newspapers pub-lish select realty transactions. Friends and neighbors then know what you bought, how much you paid, and the method used to finance. People make livelihoods reading legal notices. When your name is on legal records, you may find yourself solicited by insurance salesmen and all sorts of contractors.

With property in a corporate name the only thing that gets pub-lished is the purchasing corporation's name which is of little value to most people.

Liability. A corporation can shield individuals from certain liabilities. If a corporation has only a single asset, that generally is the only asset "at risk." Risk is minimized here too, because there is usually a record-ed mortgage which has priority over subsequent claims.

Often you will hear the expression, "piercing the corporate veil." A plaintiff's attorney might try to go beyond the corporate assets and sue the owners, directors, or managers personally. The "corporate veil" can be "pierced" where the company was fraudulently created, where corporate formalities were ignored, or where corporate officers exceed their corporate capacity.

> *Example 1*: Acme Apartments, Inc., is a corporation that functions without corporate minutes, properly issued stock, corporate tax returns, bank accounts, annual meetings, or corporate resolutions. Acme's corporate veil can probably be pierced, thereby exposing shareholders and directors to liability.

> *Example 2*: Jones, president of Acme Apartments, Inc., unlawfully batters a tenant. Tenant sues Jones who claims that the *corporation* should be sued. The case will probably go against Jones. In battering the tenant, Jones acted as an individual and outside his corporate capacity.

Transferability. If property owned in an individual's name is sold to another individual or corporation, a transfer takes place.

> *Example*: If Elaine sells her $100,000 property to George, transfer taxes are paid on this transaction because title transfers from Elaine to George.

When property is owned by a corporation it may be easier to transfer ownership through a sale of stock or through sale of the entire corporation. Transfer taxes are avoided because title has not changed. There was no transfer of title, i.e., the corporation still owns the subject property.

> *Example*: Elaine owns all the shares of ABC, Inc., which owns a $100,000 property. Elaine sells her *shares* to George. Transfer taxes are avoided because title has not changed: ABC, Inc., still owns the house. Only ownership of ABC, Inc.'s corporate shares has changed.

> *Note*: If you are fortunate to have both a lawyer and an accountant, make sure *both* professionals agree to your start-up plan. Otherwise, at tax time your accountant will berate you for not going, say, Sub-Chapter S or for not using a close corporation.

Your lawyer might berate you for having entered a general partnership when you should have entered a limited partnership. After-the-fact changes are expensive. If you have an accountant and lawyer, get them to concur at the beginning.

Disadvantages to incorporating

Start-up. It costs money to incorporate. Also, most jurisdictions charge yearly incorporation fees.

Non-acceptance. You may consider your operations corporate, but banks and stores do not generally extend credit to new corporations without an owner's personal guaranty.

Bookkeeping. Corporations require corporate identification numbers and separate tax returns. Corporations also require formality, i.e., corporate resolutions for assuming loans, valuing shares, etc. Failure to observe formality can expose owners and officers to the corporate debt.

Insurance. Insurance companies recognize that individuals sometimes own second homes and small numbers of investment properties. They consider this normal risk. Property held in a corporate name denotes commercial use, and some insurance companies do not write policies for property held in a corporate name.

Self-representation. Landlords who are not lawyers may represent themselves in court as private individuals. Problems sometimes arise when property is owned by a corporation. When landlords are not lawyers, some judges will not allow landlords to represent the corporation's interest, even if the landlord wholly owns the corporation! This may entail having to hire a lawyer in situations in which a lawyer is not really needed.

Living trusts

Another way to own investment property is through a *living trust,* i.e., a house is owned by John Doe Living Trust. Under this arrangement, the property may fall outside of probate. Donor can use property proceeds while alive and still maintain the right to sell the house and transfer proceeds to the trust. This arrangement benefits people in higher brackets and, because it is complex, this is one of the few areas where a tax advisor/attorney should be consulted.

Eviction service

Companies in larger metropolitan areas handle evictions for landlords. In some areas, real estate agents handle this function. Fees are usually reasonable and the landlord is spared having to go to court or hiring an attorney to initiate eviction procedures.

Establish an account with an eviction service *before* beginning your landlording career. You *will* need this service. Even the nicest landlord occasionally must evict a tenant for failure to pay rent or major lease violation.

> *Note*: Eviction companies allow you to maintain your "good guy" image. *You* are not evicting the tenant; the "company" is.

Generally, you sign a power-of-attorney authorizing the eviction service to act on your behalf. You will also be asked to establish an escrow account from which court costs and other fees are drawn.

> *Reality*: These companies are not your lawyers. They do not represent landlords in situations where tenants countersue, for example, on the need for repairs. When tenants countersue, companies try to obtain a postponement so that the landlord or his representative can present the landlord's case.

If eviction services are not available in your area, it pays to investigate eviction court procedures for an idea of what you might be up against. An even better idea is for new landlords to spend a morning in rent court just to see how the system works.

Property registration/licensing

In some communities rental properties must be registered with an annual fee paid. Some jurisdictions require landlords to have a rental license to collect money. Judges notoriously use rent proceedings to check landlord compliance with local property registration and licensing laws. Landlords going to court for rent are sometimes surprised when hit with fines and fees. The time to learn about property registration and licensing requirements is not in rent court.

Should you get a post office box?

For those who don't already have post office boxes, the answer is no. Box rentals are costly and so is gas to the post office. Post office boxes are time-consuming and inconvenient. While rent is due on the first of the month, checks invariably filter in a few days before and after coming due. With a rented post office box, you will find yourself making many trips to the post office.

Some people secure post office boxes because they don't want tenants to know where they live. Landlords who demand such privacy should not be in the landlord business. I am not advocating opening your living quarters to tenants, but under ordinary circumstances it is perfectly okay to have checks mailed to your house.

Should you get a separate telephone line?

If you plan to own only a few units, you can still maintain a certain degree of privacy without the expense of a separate telephone line. Most tenants respect a landlord's wishes, i.e., no phone calls past certain hours. Most tenants are comfortable leaving messages on answering machines. Some actually prefer leaving messages on answering machines.

Evening and weekend calls are inevitable. Most tenants understand a landlord's inability to secure evening and weekend repairs, but they want the landlord to be aware of the problem. And, as landlord, you should indeed be aware of what is happening to your property.

Some otherwise frugal landlords insist on getting a separate telephone line. It can be a legitimate business expense that also allows you to keep business calls separate from private calls, especially if you don't want your three-year-old answering phones. Note, however, the special concerns of the telephone company. If the company suspects a residential line is being used as a business line, they may insist on a business billing which is usually higher than residential rates. Think twice before setting an answering machine to respond, "You have reached ABC Realty. . ." More than one angry tenant has informed the telephone company of a landlord's business use of a residential phone.

Identa*Ring/Home Business Service

In some areas of the country, telephone companies are experimenting with "Identa*Ring" type service where, for a small monthly fee, incoming business calls are directed to your home telephone and are identified as business calls by a special telephone ring. There is some uncertainty as to how monthly bills are to be apportioned for tax purposes, but for many people Identa*Ring eliminates the necessity of having to pay for a separate business telephone line. Some telephone companies offer home business service at low residential rates. With this service you get a separate directory listing and business number which rings at your home location. Business calls are distinguished by a special ring so that junior does not answer the phone if you do not wish him to.

CHAPTER 2

ACQUIRING PROPERTY:
PUTTING THE DEAL TOGETHER

Part I
Finding the Right Investment Property

Employment counselors claim most available jobs are not advertised in newspapers. The same is true for investment property. Indeed, most properties are not advertised.

Find reluctant sellers.
Take a day off and play sleuth. You might find the following reluctant sellers.

Banks. For all their scrutiny and investigation, banks are stuck with foreclosures more often than they will admit.

Some banks are less than pleased to talk about foreclosures. These banks have their own ways of disposing problem properties, and they don't like dealing with the public.

Some banks provide a full list of their problem properties and can be approached about favorable financing. Even if the house is overpriced and the bank is owed more money than the house is worth, don't give up. To get their loan back (banks like to save face), banks can be most generous with financing and terms. You have your best chance getting banks to waive points, appraisal, inspection, and all the other fees discussed in the financing section of this book.

Help the bank save face.

Example: Bank lent $50,000 on property appraised at $65,000. Buyer defaults and you want the property for $45,000.

Instead of offering the bank $45,000, (what you feel the property is worth), and securing your own 10 percent, 2-point, 30-year financing, be magnanimous and offer the bank $50,000, the amount they originally lent, but with no points, and 30-year, 8 percent financing.

In this example, at $45,000, monthly principal and interest (P&I) is $394.91, and buyer pays $900 in points. *At $50,000, P&I is $366.89, a $28 monthly savings, and no points are paid!*

Old timers. Cultivate friendships with old-timers who own real estate. Some are anxious to get out of the business. Besides a wealth of information, old-timers usually have paid-up properties and are in the best position to finance.

Owners in rent court. Spend an hour or two in rent court. (This should be required of every new landlord.) You will find landlords initiating claims against tenants, usually for rent, and tenants countersuing for repairs. Some property owners at this point are totally disgusted. With the owner in court, you have him or her at a most vulnerable point to begin your negotiation.

Divorce. Who's getting divorced? Every day, new divorces are filed. Check the prominent names against names in the property books. Do they own property? There is a good chance jointly held investment property will have to be sold.

Relatives of the deceased. It's crass and I hesitate to list this option, but there *are* people who watch the obituaries. Some call these people *vultures.* You, however, will wait a respectful amount of time before calling and will preferably use a close friend of the deceased's family to raise the subject.

Landlords with vacant houses. Landlords advertising houses for rent are vulnerable to sales pitches. Empty dwellings generate no income. Owners incur fix-up expenses, and nights and weekends are spent answering calls and showing the property.

In some areas of the country, there is an additional problem of *squatters,* that is, people who move into empty houses and who are not tenants.

> *Note:* Squatter-eviction requires the same procedures outlined in this book for tenant eviction. Shortcuts usually are not allowed.

Some owners fear vacant-house vandalism. That is precisely why owners of vacant houses should be called, not for renting, but for selling. Catch them off-guard before they have an opportunity to price the market.

Some landlords jump at the opportunity to sell.
—They may have had a bad experience with prior tenants or squatters.
—The prior tenants may have been good, but the owners are scared of renting to unknown persons.
—They are tired of showing the house for rent, and your offer to buy is a dream come true.

Finding the right vacant house
Walk or ride around the neighborhood and jot down the addresses of vacant houses you might be interested in. Some neighborhoods obviously have more vacant houses than others.

If you are working with a real estate agent, let the agent investigate ownership. Otherwise, it is a well- taken trip to the property office. Private companies in larger cities sell tax assessment books listing owners and assessed property values. At some point you may wish to get a copy.

Are vacant and boarded-up houses okay?
Houses are vacant and boarded for a variety of reasons. Some reasons have nothing to do with the house itself:
— owners' failure to obtain rehab capital
— tax sale
— inheritance dispute
— partners' dispute
— bank foreclosure.

A boarded-up house is like a surprise package. From the outside it looks decrepit and foreboding—it's *meant* to look that way.

Some boarded houses are architectural nightmares. Windows behind boards are broken, interior walls are damaged, ceilings are down, floors have gaping holes, and fixtures are broken or missing. This is not the type of house you want to start with, for obvious reasons.

But some boarded houses are pleasant surprises! Windows are boarded to insure they stay intact and the house interior remains untouched. For these houses, all that is needed is a good flashlight. Too, the good thing about these houses is that after settlement you get to keep the boards!

Note: If you are going to play sleuth, you might as well learn to break codes. For example, the age of a hot water heater can usually be determined by the first four digits, i.e., "1287" means the manufacture date was December 1987.

Fire. Nothing works better than a fire to cause a house to be sold. Owners have generally been reimbursed and often prefer cash to fixing up the property.

From the rehabbing buyer's perspective, fires are great! Good structural portions of the house often remain untouched. By the time you buy the house, all the old wiring, fixtures, decrepit walls, etc. have usually been hauled away. You do not pay for things you will have to remove. The owner discounted all of this in the price, i.e., that the house has no wiring or working fixtures. You pay only for land and frame.

Handyman specials. Handyman specials range from bare shells to houses needing cosmetic touch-up. Everyone's definition of "handyman special" differs. Don't discount a house over the phone; see it yourself. Some owners attempting to be truthful unfairly belittle their houses; in reality the houses are not so bad. More often it is the other way around—owners describe their houses as palaces needing "some" work.

Two rules govern handyman specials. Seemingly, they conflict with each other.

First, buyers tend to *over*estimate repair costs.

Example: Buyer thought flooring would cost $1,200, but by shopping around or using a different approach, buyer can lay flooring for $900.

Second, while overestimating repair costs, buyers *under*estimate *what* must be done to finish the job, and the *time* needed to complete the job.

Example: Buyer knew the outside steps needed replacing, but once replacing the outside steps, went and fixed the cracked concrete, replaced the banister and reseeded the lawn. Instead of a week to finish, it took two weeks and additional funds.

Are handyman specials wise investments?
Yes, if you:
— have access to discount supplies and materials
— have time and ability to do large portions of work yourself
— can understand and work with contractors
— plan to sell the dwelling to a homeowner
— plan to hold the property as rental property for a number of
years.

Foreclosures/auctions
These are easy words; they're in all the Get-Rich-with-Real Estate books. But *how* do you do it?
By law, auctions, especially foreclosure auctions, must be advertised. Auctions are advertised in legal publications, on the courthouse steps, and in newspapers of general circulation.
While bidders are expected to come to the auction with cash or certified checks, personal checks are sometimes accepted if prior arrangements have been made with the auctioneer or foreclosing attorney.
Nothing is predictable. A rainy day may bring many people and a sunny day few. A house may sell extremely below market value, or if the crowd is hyped, extremely *above* market value. Sometimes you are able to view the inside of the property before the auction and sometimes not. Sometimes you buy an empty house, and sometimes you are stuck having to remove squatters or former owners.
While custom varies as to who pays what, in many areas buyer pays all transfer and recording fees and assumes the tax liability as of the auction date, not the settlement date.

HUD sales
The Department of Housing and Urban Development (HUD) advertises houses for sale in almost every real estate classified section. The federal government had assured Federal Housing Administration (FHA)-approved lenders, usually banks, that mortgages for qualifying houses and borrowers would be repaid. When mortgages are not repaid, the government indemnifies lenders and takes back the property.
HUD pays agents up to 6 percent commission (you must use an agent) and also a bonus to agents when houses are hard to sell. HUD may also apply up to 3 percent of the purchase price towards buyer's

closing costs.

HUD awards the house to the person with the highest *net* offer above HUD's base amount, i.e., the minimum amount HUD established for the particular property. The point to remember is that you don't have to offer list price.

Example 1: Sally offers $36,000 for an advertised house, but expects HUD to apply 3 percent of the purchase price toward her closing costs.

Example 2: Linda offers $35,000.

Linda's offer will be accepted, assuming it exceeds HUD's base amount, because it *nets* HUD a greater sum, i.e., HUD does not have to pay any portion of the closing costs.

Property offered for sale has usually been vacant for quite some time. HUD homes come with no warranties; they are bought "as is." If the house is damaged *after* the contract is accepted, the buyer can void the contract, but the price cannot be adjusted.

HUD neither assists with financing nor allows purchasers to make repairs prior to settlement. Closing must be completed within sixty days of the acceptance date, although limited extensions are granted.

Apartment buildings

However tempted, first-time investors should delay jumping into apartment buildings and garden apartment complexes. While there is nothing wrong with these multi-unit investments, "beginner's luck" applies to poker, not real estate. You will make mistakes in the beginning; mistakes might as well be on small properties, not on large investments.

Numbers multiply for multi-unit buildings which have parking lots, storm drains, elevators, boilers, and other big-ticket items. Apartment buildings, unlike single family dwellings, require more hands-on management, i.e., landlords are responsible for trash and snow removal, fire prevention systems, lobbies, halls, security, etc.

Too, there is Murphy's Law; whatever can go wrong during initial ownership *will*. The elevator or roof, which for years was fine, somehow malfunctions during your first month of ownership, or the maintenance man who has been with the property for years suddenly decides to retire. There is no reason why the numbers should not work for apartment dwellings. However, unless you have your paperwork in order and a management team in place, apartment buildings may be overwhelming first-time investments.

Should you use a real estate agent to buy property?
Advantages
  —For the type of person who needs to be pushed, agents pressure you and eventually wear you down into making your first purchase. This may be good.
  —Agents have access to computerized multiple listing services containing hundreds of listings and information regarding the investment property.
  —Agents have connections regarding financing, appraisals, inspection, insurance, and price comparables.
  —Even though they represent sellers, agents are useful negotiation intermediaries. They prepare sales contracts and hold earnest money in escrow.

Disadvantages
  —Agents like to sell high-priced houses and look for novices who aren't familiar with property values.
  —Agents work to instill guilt. They drive you around to look at investment properties; they treat you to lunch to discuss the properties. You feel obligated to buy.
  —Property income statements agents give are sometimes worse than meaningless and border on deception.
  —Agents generally know very little about the actual property. Be wary of statements as, "I *believe* the furnace is fifteen years old." If you wouldn't accept such a vague answer from a seller, neither should you accept it from an agent.
  —Agents work for a commission which buyer ultimately pays for.
  —Agents discourage buyers from making low offers.

Example 1: No real estate agent: Seller asks $80,000, buyer offers $60,000. After prolonged negotiation, they compromise at $70,000.

Example 2: Agent: as above, seller asks $80,000 and buyer wishes to offer $60,000. Agent tells buyer not to waste everyone's time and to offer at least $70,000. After prolonged negotiation, compromise is reached at $75,000.

According to law, agents must present all legitimate offers and may not tell you what to offer seller. In the real world, despite their code of ethics, agents do exert pressure on buyers to come up with larger offers.

Beware of comps.
Comps are computer-runs real estate agents give showing sales prices for comparable area houses; i.e., if similar houses sold for $60,000, seller's $60,000 asking price for the house you are looking at is reasonable.
Agents fail to recognize that investment property cannot be compared to homeowner property. It is not apples to apples, rather apples to oranges.
Even if houses look similar from the outside, component for component, investment property is usually subordinate to homeowner property, i.e., lawn, backyard, windows, floors, doors, basement, roof, bathroom, kitchen appliances, etc. Also, comp sales prices are meaningless when sales terms are unknown, i.e., seller on a comparable house may have gotten his asking price because he financed the house at below-market rates.

Getting seller's agent to see your point of view
The following example is offered for illustration. The person who told me this is not a very honest person. You should not be bribing anybody.

> *Example*: As above, seller asks $80,000; buyer wishes to offer $60,000. It being the real world, seller's agent pressures buyer to offer $70,000. Buyer offers to privately pay agent a consolation commission on $10,000, i.e., if buyer's $60,000 offer is accepted, the agent receives commission from seller on the $60,000 purchase price, plus buyer's consolation commission in gratitude to the agent for getting seller to accept $60,000.

The point is that not only must you persuade seller, you must first sway *seller's agent* to your position. Once seller's agent sees the firmness and legitimacy of your offer, the agent will work on your behalf to pressure seller. Rather than squeeze the last dime from you, the agent will work to close the deal by pressuring seller so that the agent can move on to the next sale.

What to consider when purchasing property

Selling. Before acquiring property think of *selling.* Will this property and location appeal to others? Is the projected sales price in line with the neighborhood?

Projected expenses. New investors place too much emphasis on purchase price. Everyone wants a bargain. A house is not a bargain if soon after you take title it needs a new roof, windows, furnace or air conditioner. Price these items before making your offer. After you obtain initial financing to purchase the property, it is difficult to obtain additional financing to replace expensive items.

Cash Flow. My favorite bumper sticker reads: "HAPPINESS IS A POSITIVE CASH FLOW." I don't know how people can be talked into buying property without a decent cash flow, preferably positive.

Shrewd real estate agents can represent just about every property as having positive cash flow; i.e., if you put down a large down payment, *of course* monthly payments will be low and cash flow will be positive.

Do not expect positive cash flow your first year. Admittedly, few properties generate sufficient income to cover all expenses. Certain initial and operating expenses must come from your own pocket.

Initial expenses coming from your own pocket
   — settlement expenses, i.e., title work transfer taxes, recording fees
   — initial start-up expenses, i.e. incorporation
   — the down payment

Operating expenses you probably will have to absorb
   — mortgage principal
   — reimbursement for mileage, tools
   — capital improvements
   — "perks," i.e., that fully equipped home office and computer you always wanted, car phone, retirement plan

However, if you are going to make it in landlording, rent must *substantially* cover:

— taxes
— insurance
— interest payments
— vacancies
— utilities provided by landlord
— repairs
— collection expenses
— legal and accounting fees
— newspaper advertising and other out-of- pocket expenses.

The deal must make economic sense before you get into it. To the extent rental income falls short of covering these items, it comes from your pocket, *and you are subsidizing tenant housing.*

> *Note:* Don't expect the bank to make the financial feasibility analysis for you. Lenders care about two things: your overall ability to repay a loan and the sufficiency of their *collateral.*

What about tax savings and appreciation?
Tax savings and appreciation partially compensate for "sweat-equity," i.e., your time and labor spent on the property. To stay afloat, some people apply their tax savings and anticipated appreciation to the deficit shortfall.

> *Example:* Sharon buys a $120,000 house renting for $1,000 a month in a rapidly appreciating neighborhood.

In this simplified example, house price includes closing costs. Despite the $1,000 monthly rent, Sharon still has negative cash flow because mortgage interest alone can equal the month's rent and Sharon still has other expenses (insurance, taxes, repairs). If the negative cash flow from these other out-of-pocket expenses is, say $4,000 a year, the deal may still be good for Sharon because:
—Sharon realizes a $1,000 tax benefit on the $4,000 out-of-pocket loss if she is in a 25 percent tax bracket.
—Depreciation expense for the house and fixtures should be at least another $4,000, netting her an additional $1000 tax benefit if she is in the 25% tax bracket. (The annual depreciation expense should *exceed* $4,000 because fixtures [refrigerator, stove, air con-

ditioners, etc.] use a faster depreciation schedule.)
—If the house appreciates 4 percent a year, the house appreciates
$4,800 a year.

In this simplified example, Sharon's annual out-of-pocket loss is
$4,000 but her tax savings and appreciation amount to $6,800.
Sharon's "loss" still nets a $2800 annual *profit*.

Moreover, Sharon's slim profit increases each year. Sharon's biggest
expense, principal and interest (P&I), remains the same but rents will
rise. If monthly P&I is $1,000 and rent is $1,000, ten years from now,
P&I will still be $1,000 but monthly rent will be far greater.

Tax benefits

Tax benefits are not as generous as in prior years:
—Passive income losses for most people are limited to $25,000.
—Special capital gain rates have been eliminated; capital gains are
    treated as ordinary income (this can change only for the better).
—Depreciation schedules have been lengthened.

Nevertheless, there are still tax benefits. Tax laws change every year.
You do not buy property for only a year or two, but for a longer period. Some years will realize greater tax savings than others.

Appreciation

Property in large areas of the country has not appreciated as it did in
the 1970s and early 1980s when 10 percent annual appreciation (and
greater) was common. While 10 percent annual gains may be rare,
investment property *does* continue to appreciate.

The basic leverage principal remains.

Leverage (the ability to work largely with borrowed funds) assures
that property will remain a top investment for the next many years.

Example 1: Sam, with $20,000 earmarked for savings, realizes a 6
percent yearly return ($1,200) on his money. Sam pays 28 percent
income tax on the earned interest, and nets $864 for the year.

Example 2: Pat, with $20,000, buys a $100,000 property ($10,000
down, $10,000 in points and closing costs). If the property appreci-
ates a conservative 4 percent a year, the $4,000 unrealized first-year
gain amounts to a 20 percent annual return on Pat's $20,000 initial

investment. Tax on the unrealized gain is *deferred* until the property is sold. Depreciation probably will give Pat a paper loss, further lowering her annual tax bill.

Even if there is a slight out-of-pocket operating loss in this simplified example, Pat remains ahead as long as she keeps annual out-of-pocket losses below the $4,000 yearly appreciation.

Imperfect values

Smart investors benefit from another real estate principle: *imperfect value*. Property has no set purchase or selling price. *Smart real estate investors profit on purchase and sale.*

Example: Property "worth" $100,000 is sold by a desperate seller for $80,000. Conversely, with good marketing a seller can find a buyer willing to pay $120,000 for the very same house. In this simple example there is a $40,000 *profit spread* for a tycoon with a knack for buying cheap and selling dear.

With stock, if shares go for $100 each, a person can be the greatest negotiator, but the stock will still fetch $100 a share.

Part II

Negotiation and the Art of Bargaining:
(Be wary of these points when you are the seller.)

Ten commandments for successful negotiation

I. *Thou must have credentials.* You must establish sufficient *credentials* to assure seller he is not wasting his time. The seller must be convinced of your ability in one or more areas:

— ability to come up with a down payment
— ability to pay cash
— ability to produce good credit rating
— ability to borrow funds
— rehabilitation/renovation knowledge
— you have purchased property before
— you have relatives in the business
— knowledge of the locale.

This is your poker *ante*, or "admission card" to begin negotiation.

II. *Thou shalt set the mood.* Be calm. Be respectful. Show that you are organized. Convey that you have done this before and this deal is going to work for seller *and* buyer.

III. *Thou shalt consider seller's honor.* Never tell seller his property is not *worth* what he asks. Worth is relative. To the owner, the property *is* worth the asking price. Say, rather,
—My budget can handle only $50,000.
—Because I will need to put in x, y, and z, I can offer only $50,000.
The effect is the same, but no feelings are hurt. You are not denigrating the property, only your personal finances.

IV. *Thou shalt prolong the seller/buyer relationship as long as possible.* Police use this tactic in hostage situations. The more time hostages and hostage takers spend together, the greater the chance for ultimate success.

V. *Thou shalt wear the seller down.* Ask lots of questions. Have the seller research items for you. The more time seller invests in you, the less time he has for other buyers.

VI. *Thou shalt use a good guy/bad guy approach.* Some call it shopping with a devil's advocate. Just when seller thinks he's reached a compromise with you, your partner raises another point and the ante is lowered a bit more.

VII. *Thou shalt always have another deal going.* Seller must believe you are ready to abandon ship at all times. Never become so emotionally involved with a property that you are not in a position to walk away.

VIII. *Thou shalt remember that terms are just as important as price.* Seller expects confrontation on price. Surprise seller with price flexibility, provided your favorable terms are met.

IX. *Thou shalt be flexible.* Give in on little points. Let seller "win" on items important to seller, especially "nit-pick" items as long as you get your way on items important to you.

X. *Thou shalt, as Kenny Rogers sings, know when to fold.* Unless you *must* have a specific property, avoid dealing with difficult and inflexible sellers. With so many easy going sellers out there, there is no reason to deal with stubborn and obstinate sellers.

> *Note:* Some people are skilled at hard-line negotiation. Stubborn, obstinate sellers are a "challenge" for them. They successfully intimidate sellers and belittle seller's product. They offer ridiculously low offers and nit-pick every minor flaw. I have never been able to use this approach, but if this tactic works for you, use it!

Closing the deal
One last shot: The final squeeze.

Hard-line negotiators take one last shot after everyone has shaken hands but before the contract is signed. They want seller to throw in one more item. The item is not expensive, and if seller refuses buyer will purchase the property anyway. Seller, however, is also nervous and wants to close the deal. The seller mumbles under his breath but usually complies.

The sales contract
Two rules govern:
1) Keep it *standard*.
2) Keep it *simple*.

A new lawyer approached my friend who was selling an inexpensive property and gave him an eight-page, legal- sized, single-spaced sales contract. It was a legal masterpiece containing every possible contingency and weasel clause. Guess what? Seller took one look at the contract, crumpled it, and gave it back to buyer. He wasn't even going to read it!

Stationery stores sell standard sales contracts. They're fine to use; maybe not for million dollar deals but certainly for the average investment property.

Stick to essentials.
— *Inspection.* Is the house bought "as-is," or are you going to rely on the house passing inspection?
— *Financing.* Is the house being bought for cash, or are you relying

on bank financing? Is financing conditioned upon assuming seller's mortgage?

—*What the house includes.* The contract should specify the appliances included in the sale. If a particular item is important, put it in writing. Sellers have switched refrigerators, light fixtures, and even fireplace mantels.

Insist on a walk-through prior to closing. If you are relying on tenants' rent, put it in writing. Sellers have been known to overstate tenants' rent.

—*Escrow.* Is seller going to hold the deposit (bad practice), or a neutral third party?

—*Weasel clause (also called escape clause)*: As the name implies, buyers insert these clauses to give them a way out of the contract. Sellers do not have to accept these clauses.

—*Attorney (or partner) approval clause.* This clause lets buyer sign the contract conditioned upon attorney (or partner) approval. If buyer finds a better house, the attorney or partner finds something objectionable. Seller's attorney of course can challenge buyer's good faith, but this can get to be expensive.

—*House appraisal clause.* This clause is used when buyer needs the property appraised at a certain value to secure a loan.

—*And/or Assigns.* I heard of this one case in which buyer places the "and/or assigns" notation in the contract, but also includes a financing condition. To escape the contract, buyer assigns the contract to a homeless person who of course cannot secure financing.

Buyers use all sorts of imaginative devices to escape. They have inspectors come up with the most picky points. They go back to the bank with negative information to cause the bank to withdraw a previously approved loan commitment. Again, seller's attorney can challenge buyer's good faith, but that can be time-consuming and expensive.

Note: Sometimes, *seller* must insert an "escape clause" into the contract, particularly a clause saying, "subject to existing tenant's right of first refusal." In such cases, tenants must be offered the house at the same price and terms as the potential buyer. Some tenants have demanded that this clause be inserted in the lease. In some areas, it is local law.

Flipping

Flipping, or "flipping a contract," is selling your *right to buy* property before you actually own it. This is something the "big boys" do. It's every investor's dream.

Example: Bob secures a contract to buy a $100,000 property for $80,000. Before Bob settles on the property, he convinces another buyer to pay $90,000 for the contract. Without ever owning the house, Bob realizes a $10,000 profit!

To facilitate *flips*, buyers prepare sales contracts to read, "to John Doe and/or Assigns." This means that seller will sell the house to buyer *or* the person the buyer assigns the contract. Some buyers, especially when they get a good deal, try *immediately* flipping the contract for a higher amount. If they find another person willing to pay a higher price, it is an automatic profit without spending a dime! If not, they still have a great deal on an investment property.

CHAPTER 3

PARTNERSHIPS

How to Use Them
How to Avoid Not Being Used

If you plan to own property without a partner, you can skip Part I of this chapter. However, don't overlook Part II dealing with partner fraud. Management companies and employees are also your partners, and you can still be a victim of fraud.

Part I
Do You Need a Partner?

If this is your first venture, you are no doubt scared. Managing property can be complicated, and it helps when another person shares responsibility.

Partnership advantages
— extra borrowing power
— division of responsibilities (Each partner can be responsible for that which he is most able; i.e., repairs, bookkeeping, renting.)
— a partner's freedom to go on vacation
— partners' ability to act out good guy/bad guy roles, explained below
— lessening of liability, in theory

Partnership Disadvantages
—Liability in actuality is not lessened. Each partner is jointly and individually liable for the entire partnership debt.
—Jobs are never equally divided. One partner will always be doing more.
—Partners must concur on decisions.
—There is extra paperwork and partnership tax returns

The world has known some good partnerships: Barnum & Bailey, Sears & Roebuck and Ben & Jerry's Ice Cream. Your partnership can also be successful.

If half of marriages end in divorce, a higher percentage of partnerships similarly dissolve. As in marriage, there is no such thing as equally shared jobs. One partner always feels he or she does more. What breaks up marriages breaks up partnerships. Partners begin as friends and often end as enemies.

If your first undertaking is beyond your financial means, you may have no choice but to seek a partner. But you want your partnership to outlive your mortgage.

Partnership personality

Personality is crucial. Not everyone is partnership material. You need more than just two people willing to commit certain assets to pursue a common goal.

If you are a person who has to *control* every facet of operation, if things must be done your way, partnership is not going to succeed unless you find a compatible partner.

If you are *exacting* and must have matters absolutely right, or a person who expects things scrupulously divided down the middle, there will be problems if your partner is not of this ilk.

If you are *naive* and overly trusting, your partner may learn to take advantage of you. Ultimately, the partnership will fail.

If you are overly *distrustful* or constantly suspect other people plotting against you, ensuing paranoia will dismantle the partnership.

The proper partnership basis

The first rule is not to think of partnership as a marriage. Partnership should have no romantic aspects—it is strictly business.

Structure your partnership as a *short-term* arrangement. Instead of viewing partnership as a marriage, go back a few years and think of it as a college roommate relationship. You became roommates not out of love, but necessity. You entered a relationship knowing it will last a *finite period of time:* a semester, a year, four years. When the term ended, you parted as friends; there was no messy or traumatic divorce associated with parting.

Partners should not be picky and must be willing to overlook faults and mistakes (to a point). Partners must not "Monday morning quarterback," and should almost never criticize or use the phrase, "I told you so."

Complementary skills

Partnerships work best when partners are multi-talented. Partners should be sounding boards to each other, not each other's yes-man. When one partner gets overwhelmed with an unrealistic idea, the other partner must bring him back to reality.

Partners' skills should be complementary. Too often partners are too much alike when the partnership can better use people with *dissimilar* talents. If you are not handy, find a partner who is. If you are frequently away from home, find a partner who is home, and preferably a person who actually lives near the property.

I know a group of doctors who bought several low-income properties in partnership. The doctors would rotate responsibility for going downtown to collect rent. These were men who normally billed their time at several hundred dollars an hour. These were men who never made house calls but were now making house calls to pick up rent! The partnership was doomed to fail. And it did.

Good guy/bad guy roles

This technique was invented by car salesmen. Practiced to perfection, this skill can save your partnership money and spare you from unpleasant situations.

In car sales, managers let salesmen play the "good guy" role, while the manager plays "bad guy." Together as a team, the "good guy" and "bad guy" get you to come up with more money to close the deal.

After negotiating with the salesman who seemingly is in charge, you hear lines such as, "I must check with my manager." The "bad-guy" manager comes out and says, "No, the salesman totally overlooked X, Y, or Z." Together, the "good guy" salesman and customer negotiate with the "bad guy" manager to reach a new compromised amount. The "good guy" salesman even offers to throw in part of his commission. The customer leaves thinking he got the best price possible, while the "good guy" salesman and "bad guy" manager prepare for the next deal.

As real estate partners you will learn to do the same when buying or selling property. If you don't want to rent at a certain price, you can say you have to check with your partner. You can come back and say your partner already rented it, sold it, or said the lease can be concluded only if the renter agrees to certain additional terms.

Be on guard against the good guy/bad guy approach working against *you*, i.e., when tenants or others play one partner against the other.

To avoid this trap, stick exclusively to your assigned partnership role. Otherwise, you will get scenarios such as:

—"Oh, you're here for the rent. Last month I told your partner I would be a few days late this month." (Never should two partners separately be involved with rent collection.)

—"I'd like my carpet shampooed. Even your partner said the carpet smells funny." (Again, never should two partners separately be involved with maintenance and repairs.)

General partners

General partners share equally in the venture. Sharing includes ownership, management responsibility, profit, and loss. The general partnership agreement can be voluntary, i.e., without a written agreement.

Example: Tom and Jerry buy an investment property and each puts down a like amount. Tom and Jerry divide responsibilities and agree to equally share profit and loss.

General partners sometimes have unequal interests:
— unequal investment base
— unequal responsibility
— unequal interests in profit/loss.

Example: Tom owns 80 percent of the partnership assets and Jerry owns 20 percent. Or, Tom and Jerry have agreed that if there are profits, Tom will receive 75 percent of the profits, but if there are losses, only 60 percent.

People erroneously assume that partnership liability is limited to the amount of a partner's investment and that an individual partner's personal assets are immune. That may be true between partners themselves, but in reality, each partner is responsible for the *entire* partnership debt and liability. In practice, lending institutions often require partners to personally guarantee the *entire* loaned amount.

The key to general partnerships is that while partners between themselves can agree to certain arrangements, as to the public, each partner is jointly and individually liable for the partnership debt, even if it extends beyond the partner's initial investment.

Limited partners

Limited partners are *not* involved in day-to-day operations, and their profit or loss is specifically limited to and based upon their invested amount.

> *Example*: Jill has $10,000 and wants to join Tom's and Jerry's venture as a limited partner. In a worst case scenario, as a limited partner, Jill can lose her entire $10,000 investment, even if the partnership loss is greater. On the profit side, Jill's profit is based on her $10,000 investment and is set by a pre-arranged formula.

> *Note*: While this book down plays the need for using an attorney, limited partnership is an exception. In some instances, limited partnership can be formed only under statutory authority, and a certificate of partnership must be filed with various courts.

Limited Liability Company

The *limited liability company (LLC)* is a new cross between a corporation and a partnership. You will be reading more about this entity in the future.

The LLC is similar to the Sub-Chapter S corporation in that it combines the best attributes of a partnership where there is no income tax on the business level, and a corporation whose owners are personally shielded from claims arising out of the course of business. Unlike the Subchapter S corporation, LLCs are not saddled with many prerequisites.

Not all states recognize LLCs, and the American Bar Association is drafting a model LLC statute for use by states.

Family limited partnerships

As your holdings become greater, the need for asset protection increases. Fully funded living trusts and family limited partnerships are two sophisticated avenues of asset protection you may wish to explore. Needless to say, these routes require professional guidance.

Partnership name

Some jurisdictions require special publication or notice when a *fictitious business name* is used. A fictitious business name is a name that does not contain the name of the owners, or *all* the owners.

> *Example*: A partnership of Moe, Larry & Associates would have to file a fictitious name statement if it did not include Curly, the third partner's name. Similarly, a partnership of three individuals would have to file a fictitious business name statement using the name Moe, Larry, Curly and Associates. "And Associates" implies additional partners involved in the venture.

A limited partner cannot use his last name in the partnership name unless it is also a general partner's last name.

Do you need a formal partnership agreement?

Advice books say yes and to get a lawyer. Advice books do not distinguish between a first-time, single venture between friends, as your first investment will probably be, and multi-million dollar transactions between strangers.

For those viewing partnership as marriage, a partnership agreement is akin to a pre-nuptial agreement reeking with mistrust and sowing seeds for eventual discord.

Common sense dictates that the more at risk, or if more than two partners are involved, greater is the need for a formal partnership agreement.

Partnership agreements set forth each partner's rights and responsibilities, how partnership interests are transferred, survivorship, indemnification, disclosure, dissolution, arbitration, etc.

You will read of enduring partnerships founded on no more than a handshake. Conversely, you will read of court fights where partners battle over items contained in 300-page partnership agreements that were to have provided for every contingency and ambiguity.

I personally have never used a formal partnership agreement, although I have seen them used. My reasoning is that I have carefully selected my partner and our arrangement is built on a certain amount of trust.

There are obvious risks. What happens when my partner and I disagree? Should we each carry insurance to protect the other? What happens if we decide to take on a new partner? What happens if my partner decides to enter a competing business? What happens if my partner no longer fulfills his responsibilities? What if my partner wants the partnership dissolved or dies?

These are real questions you hope will never come up or that you will be able to successfully deal with when they arise.

What I have used is a variation of the two options:

Have a partnership agreement but neither party sign it.

Find a sample partnership agreement in a library, photocopy it, and have both parties look it over with each partner keeping a copy in a drawer. The sample agreement contains common contingencies relating to obligations and responsibilities discussed above. It also can specify each partner's share of income, gains, losses, deductions, and credits. It should have provisions relating to partnership dissolution and should preferably recommend arbitration/mediation. Use the written agreement as a basis for discussion. If either party has questions or reservations, hash it out before beginning the partnership.

> *Note*: While unsigned agreements do not have the force of signed agreements, the fact that the parties orally agreed to terms and conditions in an unsigned agreement may carry some weight. It is certainly better than the predominant practice of having nothing at all.

Dissolving a partnership

Partnership dissolution is normal. From the outset, partnerships are *arrangements of convenience*, not till-death-do-you-part sacraments. Since a partnership is not a marriage, there is none of the emotional and financial trauma associated with alimony, abandonment, and child support. In-laws are not involved, nor does anyone care why the partnership broke up.

Partners generally know when the partnership relationship is beginning to unfold. Usually a change of lifestyle for one of the partners is involved. There is withholding of information. Partners begin to mistrust each other. Communication lessens and little arguments become big arguments.

The question is not whether to dissolve, but how. Two recommended approaches are mediation and arbitration. Your local bar association can provide a list; my local yellow pages carry listings under both

"Arbitration Services" and "Mediation Services."

Mediation vs. arbitration

People sometimes confuse the two terms, but they are not the same. Mediation is an informal, non-binding forum focusing on compromise. Parties reserve the right for future legal action. Arbitration is more formal and rule-oriented. Decisions are legally binding and are based upon submitted evidence. "Legally binding" means the parties agree in advance that the loser will not challenge the arbitrator's decision. Courts generally uphold "legally binding" provisions and will not hear appeals except under very narrow circumstances.

Arbitration and mediation are expensive (i.e., $100+ an hour for the arbitrator/mediator's time), but parties usually split costs. Since mediation is non-binding and advisory, the necessity for each side to bring an attorney is lessened. As opposed to court litigation, issues before arbitration and mediation are resolved more quickly, with less stress, and usually at less cost.

Part II

How Do You Know When Your Partner is Cheating?
(. . . or your paid employee or management company)

Self-reflection

Before challenging your partner or management company, self-reflection is necessary. Are your "theft" standards reasonable? Allowing a partner or employee to use partnership tools and scrap material for a personal project may be viewed as "theft" by one person, but not by another.

You must communicate your feelings or you will get lines such as, "You knew what I was doing and you never said anything."

Before challenging someone else, are *you* perceived as straight and honest? Are you known to have people lie for you? Are you known to cut corners at someone else's expense? Your attitude and behavior affect partners and employees. Dishonesty ultimately works against you.

While partner fraud and employee theft is wrong, nevertheless you must ask yourself whether your partner or employee is adequately compensated. Compensation is not limited to dollars and cents. Compensation includes praise and recognition.

Are you carrying *your* weight in the partnership? Partners who feel they are being taken advantage of by you may be prone to theft. This is especially true for employees who feel they are being treated unfairly.

Cheater psychology

Advice books tell you to tolerate no fraud. If you cannot trust an employee or a partner, you should have nothing to do with him/her.

I strongly disagree. Keep the employee, management company, or partner *as long as the relationship is profitable to you.* There is a certain cheater-psychology. Lies are kept within the bounds you tolerate.

A good thing about cheaters is that they try to overcompensate in other areas, i.e., they cheat in one area, but become star-performers in other areas. They may be your best employees, and on balance, you may even be ahead! Moreover, what assurance do you have that your next employee, partner or management company will be any more competent or honest than the one you terminated?

You know your partner is cheating when:
- — your partner volunteers to accept additional responsibility, and you are slowly being phased out of management.
- — your partner develops a new life-style that eats up money: divorce, drugs, alcohol, a lover on the side. Your partner finds time and money to go on exotic vacations or pursue mid-life dreams.
- — you are so far removed from management that your partner tells you rent is one amount when it really is higher or a dwelling is empty when it is really occupied.
- — expenses in a given area mysteriously start rising, i.e., all of the sudden, your properties start needing new floors, roofs, hot water heaters, etc. A little sleuth work on your part may be required.
- — When your partner has other rental property or fixes up his own dwelling, make sure his personal receipts are not submitted as partnership receipts. Watch for "sweet heart" deals, especially

when your partner uses the same workmen and suppliers for both his personal and partnership property.

— When your partner submits higher-than-average repair bills, there is a chance he is getting kickbacks from repair persons. Take note when your partner becomes extra "chummy" with repairmen or clerks at certain stores. Be aware that "chumminess" with clerks and repairmen fosters situations where repairmen (with your partner's collusion) bill for large jobs while performing only smaller jobs.

— When you don't see items that have been paid for, there is a chance your partner returned the item to the store for cash or credit or in extreme cases even sold it for personal profit.

Keep on guard

— If you are not involved in day-to-day management, at least be involved in the accounting bookkeeping end of the partnership, i.e., review receipts. If your partner controls both management *and* bookkeeping, you are looking for trouble.

— Know what items and repairs generally cost. If stick-on floor tiles cost 69 cents each, why are you paying $1.29 per tile? Why are plumbers charging $60 for service calls when the going rate is $50.?

— Discourage your partner from "chummy" relationships with repair people. Somehow, someway, overly chummy relationships work against *you*, i.e., padded receipts, unnecessary work being done.

— Get your partner into the habit of submitting legitimate receipts. Say it's for tax purposes, which it is. Encourage your partner to use licensed service workers and to buy supplies from stores issuing *itemized* receipts. Otherwise, you will find yourself being given non-itemized receipts from greeting card stores, shoe stores, etc.

Note: It is amazing how many stores issue cash register receipts without the store's name imprinted on the receipt. If you feel you are being cheated, insist that you will reimburse only receipts containing the imprinted store name.

— Keep a written list of repairs. Why has a new roof been put on twice in three years? Find out from professionals what average house maintenance repair should be. If they tell you $50 a month, why is your management company submitting $100 a month average bills?

Combatting fraud

Stay on top of management. If your only role is financial, you will be taken advantage of. Again, advice books will tell you that employee and partner theft of even small amounts add up, as indeed they do. However, as long as the relationship is profitable to you, your job is to minimize employee and partner theft. *Ask questions, but don't conduct inquisitions.*

Example: Elaine discovers payment of duplicate $45 plumbing bills.

— Improper response: "I see you submitted duplicate $45 plumbing bills for payment."
— Proper response: "I'm having trouble understanding what these two plumbing bills are for; can you help me?"

The first statement challenges a person's honesty and puts him on the defensive. The second allows a person an honorable way out. You will never be able to totally eradicate theft. In the above example, if the person is going to lie, he can tell you the plumbing bill was really $90, of which $45 was given as a down payment, and $45 was tendered after the work was done.

The point is, *don't terminate a relationship that is still profitable to you.* You can plug up holes and institute all sorts of internal controls. However, when dealing with people who are less than saints, as soon as you plug one hole, a second hole will open up. Accept this premise as part of life.

CHAPTER 4

LEASES

Must you use a written lease?

I know of no jurisdiction requiring landlords to give written leases where the term is for a period of a year or less. Written leases are, however, *recommended* because they define everyone's responsibilities and obligations. They are particularly good for landlords because they are generally written by landlords. Provisions are usually "form" provisions that have been tried and tested through years of court cases.

Leases are also worth money. It is easier to sell a fully-leased building since it assures buyer immediate income. A lease also satisfies buyer's fear concerning the property's fitness. The property must be fit or the existing tenant would not have signed the lease. Buyer's bank, before lending money, also will wish to see written leases; it assures lender that buyer will be able to make monthly payments.

> *Example 1: No lease.* Donna earns $40,000 a year. Donna's repay ment ability will be judged at $40,000 a year. The bank gives no credit to property income not accompanied by a lease.

> *Example 2: Lease.* Donna earns $40,000 a year. Applying for a loan, Donna also submits the tenant's $6,000, 1-year lease, payable at $500 a month. Reviewing the application, the bank will probably add 75 percent of the projected lease income to Donna's earnings. Donna's repayment ability will be judged at $44,000 a year.

Sometimes, written leases make the difference between loan approval or rejection.

Conversely, leases have the opposite effect if rent is below market value or in selling a building to buyers who want vacant property.

Leases are detrimental in dealing with nuisance or judgment-proof tenants whose signatures are worthless. Judgment-proof tenants are tenants without assets; judgments against them become meaningless. Tenants like that move at will and otherwise break leases, knowing that landlords cannot reasonably sue to enforce terms.

With nuisance tenants you wish the lease never existed. Nuisance tenants are slobs or constant complainers—sometimes both. Nuisance tenants are not major lease term violators; they would be evicted if they were. They are just annoying pains in the neck.

Landlords in these situations cannot raise rent or otherwise terminate a bad occupancy that might otherwise be terminated in non-lease situations. In these instances, it is really the *landlord* who is bound.

What's the difference between a lease and a rental agreement?

A *rental agreement* is a bare-bones contract setting forth the parties' duties and obligations. It can have all the duties and obligations contained in a lease, but unlike leases which bind parties for specific time periods, rental agreements are open, or month-to-month. Where parties don't specify time, most jurisdictions confer month-to-month tenancy status.

Rental agreements also are used to supplement a lease. Rather than encumber leases, rental agreements outline in a neat, orderly fashion house rules and regulations concerning:

— additional door locks
— music and vocal lessons
— painting
— storage
— television antennas
— time when dishwasher can run
— trash disposal
— wallpapering
— what tenants can do on the lawn, etc.
— where children can play.

Besides setting forth house rules and regulations, rental agreements clarify ambiguities found in the lease and set forth additional information.

In some situations, it may be better for landlords to use rental agreements and not leases. This is especially true when landlords are uncertain of their plans for the property.

Should you use a standard lease?

"Standard" leases are fine for most situations. They are readily obtainable in stationery stores, and have been tried and tested. Because these leases are pre-printed, tenants feel more comfortable signing them.

Pre-printed leases contain the minimum information required by law, including the landlord's or representative's name, address, telephone number, and many of the clauses contained in this chapter. The lease also acknowledges receipt of rent and security deposits.

What can go in a lease?

Since a lease is a contract between adult, consenting parties, *anything* not contrary to law or public policy can go in a lease.

You can require tenants to send you birthday cards! For the privilege of renting your house, you can require tenants to wash your car every week! These bizarre examples are used to show that parties can agree to be bound by just about anything not contrary to law or public policy.

However, since leases are usually prepared by landlords, courts generally construe lease ambiguities in tenants' favor.

Plain language

If lease terms are important, make sure they are written in clear English. Tenants may claim they did not understand what they were signing. Two of the most confusing words in the English language are "lessee" and "lessor." Use "landlord" and "tenant." A growing number of states, six so far, have gone further and *require* residential leases to be written in plain language basic enough for a consumer to understand. Some states even provide for damages for non-complying leases. These states require leases to be written in a "clear and coherent manner," and that leases be "simple, clear, understandable and readable."

Important items

Use bold print for items important to you, i.e., NO PETS. This prevents tenants from claiming a clause which they did not see was buried deep in the lease.

Note: Consider having the tenant initial a clause that tenant has been offered an opportunity to review the lease with outside counsel prior to signing, but declined to do so.

If an item is important, *make sure the tenant initials the specific item.* Better yet, if the item is of special importance, i.e., automatic renewal clauses, put it on a separate page for the tenant's separate signature. The reasons for this are obvious.

Another clause worth special initialing is a pre-occupancy inspection clause. This states that tenant has found no deficiencies upon inspecting the dwelling prior to moving in. If there are deficiencies, they are specifically noted. This clause protects both landlord and tenant.

Renting to minors

When renting to minors (perhaps students) or individuals with insufficient assets, it is advantageous to have additional persons (also known as "deep pockets") co-sign the lease.

Jurisdictions define adulthood, i.e., the minimum age for leases to be enforceable. In some jurisdictions, the minimum age is eighteen, others nineteen, etc. Underage tenants can void leases. To protect themselves, landlords should require tenants to acknowledge that they are of legal age. Then, if a tenant misrepresents his age, the landlord also can void the lease.

Which names must go on the lease?

Equally important, you must ask who will occupy the dwelling, including children. Be certain the lease lists the names *and ages* of all adults and children who will occupy the dwelling.

Failure to do so can cause situations where you find all sorts of individuals, friends, and visitors spending prolonged periods in your rented dwelling.

Note: When renting to two or more individuals, married or unmarried, make sure the lease clearly states that each tenant is jointly and individually responsible for the *entire* rent.

Names are important.

For legal purposes, use the tenant's full name, but ask the tenant how he wants to be addressed. Some tenants want correspondence addressed to their legal names, some want nicknames or maiden names. Some want professional titles, others do not.

Nothing annoys people more than a misspelled name. I know one person with a confusing last name who actually throws out unopened correspondence with his name misspelled. He says he is not the addressee! This is an extreme example of intolerance, but one to be wary of.

Discard envelopes on which you make mistakes typing a person's name. It is worth the extra penny or two to give a person an envelope without a crossed over name.

Keep the names of all the people living in the rental with the rental information. Learn your tenants' names, even the children. People are impressed that you care enough to know them. In fact, you will be a better landlord when you take the time and trouble to know your tenants. (Some landlords go as far as to send birthday and anniversary cards. That may be taking it a bit too far.)

Term of lease

Residential leases are either month-to-month leases or term leases for six months, a year, two years, etc. Most jurisdictions require leases in excess of one year to be in writing. Some jurisdictions require that long-term leases, i.e., longer than three years, be recorded.

> *Note*: Long-term leases are often of marginal value and bind landlords more than tenants. Tenants who want to break a lease can make a landlord's life awfully hard. Tenant bankruptcy also can release tenants of their lease responsibility.

Be careful how you word the terms of the lease.

It's odd, but true—a lease reading, "Rent is $500 a month beginning January 1, and ending December 31," is *not* a legally binding one-year lease!

It is a month-to-month lease, where rent is set at $500 a month during the year. If the tenant leaves in September, the landlord has no recourse to enforce the lease for the remaining three months.

To make it binding for a year, the lease should read, "Rent is $6,000 *a year*, payable at $500 a month." Now if the tenant leaves in September, the tenant is responsible for the balance of the $6,000 commitment.

Watch your wording. Be positive.

Courts sometimes hold provisions contrary to public policy solely because of negative wording.

A lease providing that "leases will not be renewed for tenants failing to send landlord a birthday card" will probably be held to be contrary to public policy.

Worded differently, the provision might be enforceable, i.e., "Leases will be renewed only for tenants sending landlord a birthday card."

While the results are the same, the first wording is offensive, punitive, and socially repugnant. The second wording is elective and within the accepted scope of what parties may contract. Wording makes a world of difference to courts.

Automatic renewal

Buried in some leases are provisions that, unless tenant notifies landlord that tenant is not renewing the lease so many days or months before the lease expiration, the lease automatically renews.

Tenants do not often read fine print, and courts have problems enforcing these provisions. Some jurisdictions require landlords to notify tenants that the renewal period is coming up. Other jurisdictions require that automatic renewal provisions be distinctly set apart from the other lease provisions with space provided for separate tenant acknowledgement. This appears to be the better practice that is fairer to all.

Moving before the lease expiration

This is an important lease provision. It lets tenants know they are responsible for the unexpired term. Landlords have a duty to mitigate damage by trying to rent the apartment, but if landlords have other vacancies, they may fill them first.

The lease or rental agreement also can contain a clause recognizing that upon a breach of lease the landlord may sublet the dwelling, but if the sublessee breaches the lease or fails to pay rent, the original tenant is still liable for the rent for the remainder of the term.

Suing a tenant for an unexpired lease term is usually a waste of time and resources. Sometimes, tenants leave no forwarding address, and landlords are happy just to get the property back in reasonably good shape.

Nevertheless, the provision is recommended for honest tenants who will stand by their commitment to remain for the term, tenants of means, and tenants worried about credit ratings.

Exculpatory clauses

Some form leases contain exculpatory clauses holding landlord harmless from liability caused by the landlord's negligence. Many courts find these provisions against public policy.

Landlords often retain these vague and non-enforceable clauses, hoping tenants will not pursue further action. Too, there is always a chance the court's position will change.

Some landlords attempt to shift the burden to the tenants and impose language such as, "Tenant will hold landlord harmless from the following perils, and tenant will carry insurance of not less than such and such an amount." On damage issues, there is a greater likelihood for a court to find for the landlord when the tenant failed to obtain the required insurance.

Late payments, returned checks

Landlords put all sorts of penalties and charges into leases. Some landlords insert a "fee for default" clause, i.e., if the landlord has to resort to an attorney or collection agency to collect the rent, a 30 percent collection charge is imposed.

> *Note*: Where local jurisdictions provide a maximum amount for late charges and returned check fees, amounts in excess might not be enforceable.

Accelerated payments

Some leases provide for accelerated rent payments where tenant breaches the lease terms. In such a situation, the remainder of the term rent becomes due immediately.

Are these clauses upheld? Generally yes, under the principle that since parties can agree to have the entire rent paid in advance, parties can agree to accelerate payment of rent for a breach of the lease. Conversely, a minority of courts hold accelerated payments invalid as creating unenforceable penalties, especially when no distinction is made between major and minor breaches of lease.

Grace period

Some landlords insert five to ten day grace periods before assessing late charges. *This is not recommended.* You can voluntarily adopt this practice, but it should *not* be in writing. Some tenants habitually rely on this period. You also jeopardize your chances of evicting nasty tenants on the second or third of the month when the lease has grace period protection.

When grace periods are not written into a lease, can a landlord allow one tenant a grace period but not another tenant? The courts say yes. The decision to allow a grace period is up to the landlord.

If a landlord allows a tenant a grace period one month, does the landlord have to allow it in succeeding months? The courts say no, provided the landlord states in writing that acceptance of late payment does not relieve tenants of their obligations under the lease.

Pets

Are you going to allow pets? If so, what size pets? Are you going to require any special security deposit to insure that carpets are cleaned?

It is tempting to prohibit pets, especially when there is an apartment shortage and landlords can be choosy. During times of vacancies, landlords have to be more tolerant. Landlords also have to recognize that a rational pet policy encourages good tenants to stay. A landlord's dream is to have his dwelling occupied by a sweet, retired citizen with a little cat or puppy for comfort and protection.

> *Note:* Even with a no pets policy, there are exceptions, i.e., seeing eye dogs. Federal and state laws prohibit exclusion in most instances.

Before blindly inserting a "No Pets" provision, consider your rationale. With furnished rentals, a landlord is understandably concerned about carpeting and furniture; however, with unfurnished and uncarpeted rentals, there is less to worry about.

A better policy is to be specific as to what pets are allowed and what pets are excluded, i.e., cats, dogs, fish, birds, etc., or what size animals, i.e., no fish tank greater than thirty gallons, or pets greater than twenty-five pounds.

Don't forget the *number* of pets, or you may have a charming tenant with fifteen cats or poodles!

Waterbeds

Some landlords absolutely prohibit waterbeds. In former days, waterbeds were associated with long-haired, free-spirited, anti-war, pot-smoking hippies. Landlords did not want that sort of tenant and further feared waterbeds would cause flooding and caved-in floors.

Two decades have passed since waterbeds became popular. I know no one who even knows anyone who has ever heard of a waterbed crashing through a floor, nor have I ever heard of any major damage caused by an errant waterbed spewing liquid contents on a floor.

Growing numbers of people use waterbeds, especially middle-aged people with back problems. Waterbed salesmen claim more than 10 percent of beds sold today are waterbeds. To exclude the waterbed population is to exclude a significant portion of renters.

Noise and smell

Noise is an area of growing contention. Home music systems seem to be getting larger and more powerful, and people seem to entertain at home a lot more these days.

As landlord, you will get complaints from other tenants and from adjacent homeowners. Some complaints are serious: banging at all hours of night, wild midnight parties. Some complaints are less serious: musical instruments, early morning showers, excessive bathroom use.

No lease can list *every* possible form of tenant disturbance, although some landlords try. Their leases contain provisions regarding singing lessons, phonographs, musical instruments, and radios. Their leases contain permitted times for running the garbage disposal, washing machine, dishwasher, and television.

Your lease *should* contain *general* noise provisions, i.e., "Tenants shall not make or permit any disturbing noises, nor do or permit anything by such persons as will interfere with the rights, comfort, or convenience of other tenants." However, only in the most severe instances should you get involved in noise disputes, and even then you would be better off staying out. Your taxes support the local police whose job it is to keep the peace. Landlord intervention in noise disputes is a lose-lose proposition.

The same is true for tenant disturbances through smell. It is one thing for garden apartment leases to prohibit outdoor barbecues, which many apartment leases do. But it is another thing to prohibit ethnic cooking whose smell may offend other people. Landlord intervention in these disputes is a lose-lose proposition.

Floor coverings
Where tenants live above other tenants, you may wish to require carpeting for a certain percentage of each floor, i.e., 75 percent, (excluding bathrooms and kitchen). This keeps noise down. While landlords benefit by tenants investing money in the apartment because of the outlay of funds required, such policies, if enforced, reduce the number of available tenants.

Drapes, laundry, and window ornamentation
Some landlords restrict the types of window drapes and window ornamentation. Landlords do this to promote aesthetic uniformity. Be careful. Some restrictions make sense, i.e. restrictions against business signs hanging from windows. But some landlords face difficulty when first amendment issues are involved, i.e., flags or other forms of protected speech.

> *Note*: Make sure your rules provide that nothing can be hung out of windows or you may find situations where tenants air out sheets and quilts from windows. Similarly, if your rules or local jurisdiction does not allow washed clothing to be hung outside to dry, this restriction must be noted in the rental agreement.

Improvements
The lease should contain provisions requiring tenants to obtain permission before installing fixtures or making "improvements." A tenant-installed light fixture is dangerous if it was installed incorrectly. It can cause a fire or crash on someone's head. This ultimately becomes your responsibility.

> *Note*: Sometimes landlords grant permission conditioned upon the improvement remaining on the property, i.e., paneling or mirrored walls where removal would damage the walls.

Alterations

Along with provisions requiring landlord approval for improvements, leases also should require landlord approval for alterations.

> *Note*: Handicap discrimination laws sometimes require landlords to allow alteration of the premises at tenant's expense, i.e., widened doorways, lowered light switches, wheelchair ramps, etc. These laws require that premises be returned to its prior condition at the termination of the tenancy, especially when the alteration interferes with the next tenant's use of the property.

Repairs

A good lease contains repair-notification requirements. Delays in reporting repairs can necessitate larger repairs. Delayed repairs can cause accidents. This is a landlord defense if there is an accident and the tenant failed to inform a landlord of needed repairs.

Some leases prohibit tenants from making their own repairs. Tenants are usually unskilled and unlicensed. Tenants often lack the correct tools needed for proper repairs and may use inferior or incorrect materials, i.e., using aluminum electric wire in a copper-wired house can cause a fire. All sorts of liability issues arise if the tenant's repair is negligent.

Dollar repair requirements

Some landlords, especially landlords with only one or two rental units, put $40 dollar repair requirements (or similar amount) in their leases. This clause has tenants responsible for repairs under a certain amount. Besides cost savings, landlords do this for several reasons:

—Since most repairs are minor, landlords are not bothered with minor problems.

—Tenants responsible for minor repairs will think twice before calling for repairs.

—Tenants are responsible for calling the repair person, being home for repairs, and making sure that repairs are correctly done.

This clause works best when single-family rental houses are involved, as opposed to apartments where occupancy is often of shorter duration. Too, it works best when the tenant rents a relatively new house where repairs are not a normal occurrence.

The drawback against a tenant dollar repair requirement is that when rent payments are high (as it should be), tenants expect rent to include repairs.

Landlords also run the risk of tenants failing to make timely repairs. When the repairs are finally made, they become more costly.

Business

The lease should contain provisions prohibiting the premises from being used as a business. Landlord liability insurance covers only tenant's guests, not their business patrons.

Security deposits

Some jurisdictions allow landlords to collect more than just one month's rent as a security deposit. Some limit security deposits to not more than two months' rent.

To avoid the bookkeeping hassle involved with security deposits, some landlords credit the security deposit toward the last month's rent. This is *not* recommended.

A security deposit is not only to assure the landlord the last month's rent, but also that the dwelling is left in decent shape and all other agreements are fulfilled. If a tenant knows money is coming back if the dwelling is left in decent shape, he will work to get the deposit back. If the deposit is only for the last month's rent, there is no incentive to clean the dwelling before leaving.

> *Note*: Calling a security deposit pre-paid rent for the last month of tenancy also has tax implications, i.e., it immediately becomes earned income.

Commonly asked questions

If a tenant fails to pay rent in the middle of the term, can a landlord evict a tenant who has the last month's rent paid? The courts say, yes. The tenant can be evicted, especially when the lease states that the pre-paid last month's rent is not only for the term's last month but also to assure compliance with all other conditions in the lease.

If a tenant goes bankrupt, does the landlord have to tender the security deposit to the bankruptcy trustee? The courts say, no. The landlord can continue to hold the security deposit for the faithful performance of the lease agreements.

Other security deposits
Some landlords impose additional security deposits for:
— pets
— air conditioners
— water beds
— water, utility bills
— cleaning.

Some landlords impose additional "key deposits," i.e., for return of keys. If you adopt a cylinder rotation policy after each tenancy, you do not really need your keys back. Key deposits will be one less charge to worry about.

Some landlords impose an additional $75 security deposit to assure that the rental, particularly the bathroom and kitchen, is left clean.

Security deposits are more easily said than done. As rents rise, it is harder for landlords to collect security deposits. You will see many newspaper ads advertising 0, half-month or $250 security deposits for "qualified people."

As an aside, I am amazed at the gall (or genius) of No-Money-Down gurus. An idea I just read is to advertise a house for rent *before* buying it, interview prospective tenants, and ask for (and receive) three *months'* security deposit which the No-Money-Downer uses for closing costs! No comment.

Back to the real world, some landlords waive security deposits for older tenants. This apparently does not run afoul of discrimination laws. Few landlords today enjoy the luxury of collecting all necessary security deposits.

> *Note*: As an alternative to collecting miscellaneous security deposits over and above the regular security deposit, the lease or rental regulations should contain a list of fees that will be charged for lost keys, and kitchens and bathrooms left in a slovenly manner, etc. There is no assurance that the fees can be collected but it informs tenants of your standards and their responsibility.

Right of distraint

This clause allows landlord to keep tenant's possessions and store or sell them if rent is not paid. It's rare that tenants just disappear leaving a house full of furniture and possessions, but it does happen, and distraint clauses as security for rent are helpful.

> Note: Distraint clauses are generally accompanied by a *right-of-possession* clause allowing the landlord to reenter the dwelling, store or sell the property, and most importantly, rent the dwelling to another.

Eviction

An eviction clause is inserted to inform the tenant that eviction and reentry can be sought not only for failure to pay rent but for violation of *any* lease term.

Damages

Landlords should insert a clause stating that tenants inspected the premises prior to renting and found no defects. Damages or pre-existing defects should be in writing to protect both parties in the event of disputes.

Landlords and tenants each have the right to demand to be present when the tenant leaves to check the premises. This protects tenants who can get the landlord to sign that the premises are vacated in a satisfactory condition. It assures landlords that the premises have been vacated properly. The prudent landlord then changes the lock.

> Note: While landlords would like to withhold security deposits for every mark on the wall that must be painted, courts generally allow tenants "ordinary wear and tear." While decent tenants spackle walls where pictures hung, tenants are ordinarily under no obligation to spackle walls.

Return of security deposit

Local laws are very exacting as to return of security deposits and interest where applicable, and often impose punitive damages on landlords who fail to return deposits by a given time.

Landlords who deduct from a tenant's security deposit are also under an obligation to inform tenants of the damage or claims for which the security deposit is being withheld. A landlord has the right to expect a forwarding address from the tenant.

> *Note*: Some jurisdictions do not require interest when tenants occupy a premises for less than a year. Some jurisdictions impose an interest requirement only when the landlord has a certain number of rental units or a prescribed number of rental units in a single building.

Landlord's right-of-entry

This usually is not a problem. Tenants *want* the landlord to enter the property to do needed repairs.

Nevertheless, the lease or rental agreement should contain right-of-entry provisions specifying that repairs will be performed during business days and during waking hours, i.e., between 9 a.m. and 8 p.m., and that appliances may be shut off during repairs.

> *Note*: Landlords must have the right to enter the rental if only to inspect the property. Some of the larger cities are beginning to crack down on *landlords* where drugs and illegal tenant activities take place.

Door locks

To preserve the landlord's right-of-entry, leases should provide that if tenants change entry locks, and particularly if tenants install second locks, i.e., dead-bolts, landlord must be given a set of keys.

Notice

Tenants may insist upon notice before landlord or his workman enter the leased premises. While this is a reasonable request, it is not always practical.

It is hard to get repair people to commit themselves to a specific time, and sometimes repairs must be done while tenants are away, i.e., on vacation. If your policy is to use only licensed and bonded repairmen, this might reassure a tenant that his/her possessions will remain untouched.

As a point of law, landlords have a right to enter the premises for maintenance checks and repairs. Obviously, this right must be reasonable and does not extend to midnight hours, etc.

Careful landlords may wish to consider having tenants sign a waiver recognizing landlord's right to enter, and specifically waiving any right to notice.

Landlords also may wish to impose reentry provisions to show the house or apartment (during business days, and daytime hours) if tenant has notified landlord that he is terminating or otherwise not renewing the lease.

Again, the majority law is on the landlord's side. Courts have held that a landlord is allowed to place a "For Rent" sign in the tenant's window, especially when tenant has given a notice to vacate. Courts have held tenants liable for failing to afford landlord a reasonable opportunity to show the leased premises.

But as above, while the law is on the landlord's side, it is best to put it in the lease.

Insurance

The lease should contain an insurance provision clearly informing tenants that landlord does not carry insurance for tenants' personal belongings. This usually becomes a problem when water damages tenants' belongings. Some insurance policies cover situations where water damage is external, i.e., water seeping in from the outside; some only from acts of God; and some cover situations where damage is from internal sources, i.e., a busted water pipe.

A really careful landlord might consider having the tenant initial that tenant understands that insuring tenants' possessions is the tenants' responsibility.

Acts by landlord's employees

Questions always arise about landlord liability when a tenant's property is wrongfully harmed by the landlord's employee or repair person.

Courts surprisingly often rule in the landlord's favor and hold the landlord responsible only for gross negligence, willful conduct, or fraud, not ordinary negligence. The tenant may have a claim against the perpetrator, but not against the landlord.

A careful landlord may even wish to put this in the lease. It sounds like an exculpatory provision that will not be enforced. Indeed, there may be jurisdictions that will not enforce it. But since there are jurisdictions that *may* enforce it, and since laws always change, it is worth having.

Owner's representative
Be careful when using form leases that contain absolutely no owner information. Besides often being required by law, it is to everyone's interest for the lease to contain the owner's mailing address and telephone number.

Legal fees
You may want a paragraph inserted advising tenant that if the landlord has to incur legal fees to enforce tenant compliance with lease provisions, legal fees will be paid by tenant.

Failure to give tenant possession
You want a paragraph inserted holding landlord harmless if he is unable to give a tenant possession of the property on the lease date.

Example: Tenant A informs landlord he will vacate by November 28. Landlord gives Tenant B a lease beginning December 1. Tenant A does not move out by the twenty-eighth and has to be evicted. Tenant B sues landlord for not having the apartment ready by December 1. While the landlord might be protected even without such a paragraph, insertion puts Tenant B on notice that a possibility exists that landlord might not have the premises available on the scheduled date.

Some landlord leases contain provisions requiring new tenants to inform the landlord *in writing* that they are not taking the apartment because of the landlord's inability to tender the apartment, and that barring such written notification, the new tenant's rent obligation will begin as soon as the landlord is able to tender possession.

Example: Prior tenant leaves on the twenty-eighth of the month, but the landlord is not able to get the dwelling in shape until after the first of the month. Unless the new tenant informs landlord in writing that he is not taking the apartment, the new tenant's responsibility begins when the landlord tenders possession to the new tenant.

Failure to give landlord possession
What do you charge a holdover tenant, especially when the holdover delays a new tenant's occupancy?

Holding over can even cause the new tenant to find different accommodations. Some states allow landlords to assess double rent to holdover tenants. Your lease can specify even greater damages.

Prohibited provisions
  Jurisdictions and courts vary, but most will not enforce:
  — retaliatory provisions allowing landlord to evict a tenant for joining a tenant's organization or complaining to a housing authority
  — provisions whereby tenant waives his right to remedies provided by law
  — provisions whereby tenant waives his right to allow certain individuals on the premises. (Commercial leases may include such provisions, i.e., the landlord can prohibit a tenant from allowing peddlers and solicitors from entering a property.)

Lease with an option to buy
  Some landlords insert this clause, which, as its name implies, gives tenants the right to buy the house at a set price. Some landlords even credit a certain portion of the rent toward the purchase price.
  The companion clause is a *tenant's right of first refusal*, which lets tenants purchase the house at the same price and at the same terms offered to another buyer. [In some areas, tenants in single-family houses have this right as a matter of law.]
  Some experts recommend against inserting these clauses into leases. There is a certain logic to their objection.
  —A lease with an option to buy is one sided, i.e., tenant is under no obligation to exercise his right to purchase, but landlord is bound to a certain purchase price. If the house appreciates greatly in value, the landlord is bound to the contract price.
  —Crediting a portion of the tenant's rent toward the purchase price in actuality is a rebate and monetary gift that diminishes the price the landlord receives for the house.
  Sometimes, these clauses benefit the landlord:
  —In some instances, it is the difference between a tenant taking a house or not. Landlords want not just any tenant, but the *right* tenant. You want tenants with home-ownership ambition.
  —Tenants protected by these clauses are apt to stay longer.
  —Tenants protected by these clauses are apt to view the house as

their own, especially regarding improvements and repairs.

Obviously, the contract price set by the landlord takes all the objections into consideration.

Must a lease be witnessed and notarized?
As a general rule, no. Landlord and tenant signatures are sufficient. Where leases exceed a year, some states require witnesses and acknowledgement (notarization). Some states require witnesses and notarization only where leases exceed three years.

> *Note:* People often ask what "(SEAL)" after the signature space means and whether the lease is enforceable if "(SEAL)" is omitted?

SEALs are archaic and their required usage mostly has been abolished. Justice will still prevail if the SEAL is omitted. SEALs are used today primarily to impress the signatories as to the significance of their action.

LEASE/RENTAL REGULATIONS CHECKLIST

Items to consider

— clause that tenants are of legal age
— clause that lease is binding on tenants (jointly and individually), their successors and representatives, i.e., if they die, you want the estate to pay off the term
— clause that rental is for a term of years payable over so many months
— clause that landlord does not send out special rent notices
— clause concerning landlord's possible failure to tender possession
— clause that the lease is a legal document and tenants are advised to consult a legal authority if they have any doubts
— clause that tenants have inspected the property before renting it and have found everything in order
— clause requiring tenants to notify landlord of any structural or mechanical defects
— clause that landlord has the right to shut off equipment when necessary for repairs, etc.

— clause that, in the event of fire, landlord has the right to repair dwelling or terminate tenancy
— clause that landlord is not responsible for damages caused by the disruption of service, unless willfully caused by landlord
— clause that tenant will not do anything to jeopardize landlord's insurance
— clause that tenant will do nothing unlawful, i.e., grow marijuana
— clause that waiver by landlord of any specific term of lease does not imply that landlord will waive specific performance in the future
— clause setting forth how communication is to be made, i.e., regular or certified mail
— pets restrictions, if any
— names and ages of all tenants, including children
— exculpatory clauses
— late payments, late charges, returned checks
— fee-for-default clause
— where and how rent is to be paid
— grace period
— eviction
— fees and damages for holding over
— right of distraint
— parking
— use of storeroom or common areas
— trash
— door locks
— noise and quiet enjoyment (general)
— musical instruments, etc. (specific)
— TV antennas
— waterbeds
— barbecues
— utilities—who pays what
— floor coverings
— contact paper on walls
— drapes, laundry, window signs, and ornamentation
— improvements, alterations, repairs
— dwelling purposes only, i.e., no business
— improvements, alterations, repairs
— dollar repair requirement

— landlord's right-of-entry
— notice
— insurance
— owner's representative
— legal fees
— option to purchase
— automatic renewal
— security deposit(s): for rent; air conditioners; water beds; water; utility bills; cleaning; legal; eviction fees; keys
— subletting: restrictions—for or against

CHAPTER 5

TENANT SELECTION

*"Good tenants are hard to keep...
bad tenants are hard to get rid of."*
— Anonymous Property Manager

Renting is salesmanship
Tenant selection involves more than just the initial "sale." You have to *live* with the tenant for the duration of the tenancy. Renting a dwelling to another person involves salesmanship. If your rent is too high or your house is not in the best location or condition, all is not lost.

The decision to rent is based on three factors: price, condition, and location.

But emotion can overpower logic, especially when the landlord is warm, interested, and caring. Sometimes, a warm, interested, and caring landlord is the most important factor to a prospective tenant.

A way of life
Remember you are not merely selling a four-walled dwelling of bricks and mortar, you are selling *a way of life* comprised of safety, convenience, prestige, cleanliness, and comfort.

Think of prospective tenants as friends you want to help. Think why renting the house is in the tenant's best interests, not only your own.

Renting Do's and Don'ts
When showing a dwelling, be positive and cheerful. Dress well. A neat appearance attracts neat tenants. Be honest about the house condition, but don't unnecessarily degrade it. Be enthusiastic, and of course, accentuate the positive.

Ask a prospective tenant if he likes to garden. If the answer is yes, show off the garden and direct the conversation toward gardening. If the answer is no, drop the subject. To some people a garden is an asset, to others a burden.

Show the house during the best time of day. Some houses show better at night. If you want prospective tenants to see children on the block, show the house during hours neighborhood children are at play.

Conversely, if daytime parking is limited, or there is some other daytime inconvenience, avoid showing property then. If existing tenants are unkempt, you may want to wait until they are away to show the property.

Experts recommend a warm and comfortable atmosphere. They recommend soft music and delicious odors emanating from the oven. You can do that with an occupied dwelling but not when the house is vacant. But try. If the house power is on, turn on *all* lights. Similarly, turn up the air conditioning or heat. It shows prospective tenants that all systems are working, and that you the landlord are not cheap.

> Note: To get an extra bright look, increase the wattage on all bulbs. No one likes viewing a dingy house or apartment.

When showing an empty house, make sure light bulbs are put back (sometimes they have been removed); that toilet paper is on the spool; and that paper towels are on the kitchen paper-towel rack. We are not talking serious money here. It is the least you can do to make a vacant dwelling look livable.

Don't unnecessarily label prior tenants deadbeats, or prospective tenants will think you attract that sort of tenants. Speak glowingly of prior tenants. Give prospective tenants models they will have to live up to.

Not every tenant who sees your house will want to rent it. Be prepared for rejection and accept it positively. As my cousin says: "Sometimes the best rental is the rental you *didn't* make."

Sometimes, people call months later asking if the place is still available. They liked you or the house, or both. Take it as a compliment.

On the other hand, not every tenant can make on-the-spot decisions. Tell prospective tenants you will call them. Don't pressure them. But as a salesman, don't wait for them to call you.

Karma

Houses, even rental ones, have a certain *karma*. Just as you would prefer renting a house where prior occupants had charmed, beautiful lives, i.e., people who have not met misfortune, prospective tenants also want assurance that prior occupants were straight, normal, and happy people. Similarly, prospective tenants want assurance that you as landlord are straight, normal, and happy. Assure them.

AIDS, murder

The law is mixed on whether one must tell prospective tenants or buyers about matters unrelated to the physical property, i.e., renting or selling a house where a person was murdered or died of AIDS.

Where the prior occupant was murdered or committed suicide, there seems to be an obligation to disclose, although many states have passed disclosure laws that for the most part classify murders and suicides as "non-material" facts. As for AIDS and other diseases, there are rulings that unsolicited disclosure is in fact *illegal*.

Ghosts

Ghosts are somewhere in between. A recent New York appeals court ruled that sellers were obligated to disclose the alleged condition to buyers.

Problem tenants

Problem tenants are tenants you wish on your worst enemy. You only wish they broke the lease terms so you could evict them. But they haven't. Nevertheless,

—Rent is paid late.
—They are slobs.
—They are noisy.
—They lie.
—They attract all sorts of visitors.
—They complain about every minor thing.
—They call housing inspectors before calling you.
—They call at all hours of the night.
—They expect repairs within minutes.
—Nothing fixed manages to stay fixed.
—They bad-mouth you to other tenants.

No landlord can honestly admit to never having such tenants. But much can be done to lessen the odds of a house being occupied by harassing deadbeats.

Credit checks
Advice books recommend checking tenants' income and assets, but they never tell you how.

The easy answer is that, in most cities, you can subscribe to a credit service. For an extra fee, some credit bureaus also will analyze applicant's record for you. There is a cost/benefit analysis. These services are neither cheap nor always accurate. Ideally, prospective tenants pay for credit reports. Since this is more easier said than done, landlords sometimes are left with the tab.

> *Note*: You also may have to wait several days for the credit bureau report. This puts you at a disadvantage, especially when tenants are also looking at other properties. (A fax machine can sometimes speed things up.)

Too often, there is insufficient information to make a proper determination. This is especially true for immigrants, newly divorced or young people who have not yet established credit.

Most likely, you are going to have to conduct your own search and ultimately rely on gut feelings. There will be instances where your best paying tenants are those who *failed* a credit check and your worst paying tenants those who *passed*.

Tenant application form
Whether or not you perform credit checks, there is no excuse for not having a tenant application form. Applications help you evaluate tenants for selection, but equally important, provide information needed when things go bad.

Sometimes, tenants disappear. You call for your rent and get a recording that his phone is temporarily disconnected. You knock on his door, but no one is home. You call his job only to find he no longer works there.

All is not lost. Go back to your tenant application form which has information pertaining to your tenant's friends and relatives. *They* still have phone service and may know whether your tenant took an extended vacation or what. You can leave messages for your tenant through them.

You also have your tenant's Social Security number and driver's license which sometimes can be of great value.

Should you make up your own application form?

Think twice before drafting your own application form. Use standard forms available in office supply stores. Why?

In this day and age of discrimination lawsuits, you don't want to ask improper questions. While it's your business to know how many people will occupy your dwelling, questions concerning marital status may be improper. While you may ask if the tenant is of lawful age, general questions concerning age may be improper, as well as questions concerning education or arrest records.

> *Note:* While you can't ask whether a tenant has ever been arrested, you may ask whether a tenant has ever been *convicted* of a crime. The reason for this difference is that not everyone arrested is convicted, i.e., some people are found innocent.

Past residence

Actually, information concerning past residence is of limited value. Landlords with rotten tenants are only too happy to rid themselves of such headaches. What do you imagine a landlord with a bad tenant is going to say? Of course you are going to get a favorable recommendation especially if it gets the tenant out of his/her house and into yours.

If you are going to question a current landlord, don't ask general questions such as, "Is Mr. X a good tenant?" It is easy to hedge on general questions. Hedged answers might be, "I can't begin to tell you what a fine person Mr. X is," or, "I can't say enough about Mr. X." What exactly does that mean?

Ask the landlord specific questions requiring a yes or no answer. Honest people find it hard to lie, and you can tell when they give hesitating, roundabout answers.

—"Has Mr. X been late with rent more than two times?"

—"Did you ever send a rent notice to Mr. X?"

—"Have neighbors ever complained to you about Mr. X?"

It probably makes more sense to speak to the prospective tenant's *prior* landlord, not the current one. Prior landlords can be more truthful since they don't have to worry about getting problem tenants to leave.

Moreover, there are three important question which only prior landlords can answer, and current landlords cannot:

— whether the tenant broke the lease or failed to give proper notice
— whether the tenant left owing rent
— whether the tenant left the dwelling in a satisfactory condition.

Too, don't forget to ask the prior landlord the most important question which embraces all aspects of the landlord-tenant relationship:
—"Would you rent to Mr. X again?"

> *Note*: In some areas a call to the local police can be helpful. Police keep complaint logs by address, i.e., did complaints to police originate from tenant's last address?

Visiting tenant's prior address

Advice books recommend actually visiting the tenant's current address. Where practical, that makes certain sense. It shows the tenant that you care about cleanliness and neatness.

But looks can be deceiving. A tenant's neat house is no guarantee that rent will be paid on time, that tenant will not be a landlord harasser, or that there won't be disruptive parties, etc.

Employment

Don't be fooled by a tenant's employment record. It tells you nothing about how a tenant pays his rent, or what kind of tenant he is. Again, ask the employer specific questions, i.e., "Have you ever had to garnish Mr. X's wages?"

Employment information gives you insight as to how long tenant may stay. Employees in certain jobs, such as the military, transfer quite frequently. You may or may not want such individuals as tenants.

> *Note*: Various federal and state laws govern the military, especially servicemen called for active duty. You may not want to be locked in a situation where you cannot evict a tenant because he or she is on active duty.

Some landlords ask prospective tenants point blank how long they intend to stay. They may get lies, but sometimes they also get the truth.

Formulas

Employment information provides insight into whether a tenant can afford to rent your dwelling. Experts generally recommend a certain percentage of a person's gross income (from all sources, i.e., salary, alimony, interest, etc.), that can comfortably go for rent (between 25 and 30 percent).

Before getting carried away analyzing percentages, realize that in actuality there are no hard and fast rules. No formula actually determines how a tenant pays his rent. There are tenants awash with money who drag out rent payments and tenants with limited resources who never miss a payment. Use employment/income data only as a guide— *one* of your guides in tenant selection.

Select tenants carefully.

Rented premises are sometimes used for gambling, drugs and the illegal storage of toxic waste.

The age of innocence is over. Jurisdictions increasingly look to landlords to monitor illegal activity. In a recent case, a landlord at a self-storage warehouse paid a $200,000 fine to clean up a tenant's mess caused by 1,000 pounds of toxic pollutants. The caveat to know your tenant, and for what purpose the leasehold is being used, is as true today as ever.

> *Note*: To guard against a leasehold being improperly used, landlords must retain periodic inspection rights and copies of all keys to the premises.

Newspaper ads

Which newspaper?

Landlords advertise in two types of newspapers: daily and Sunday. The number of ads in the Sunday classified "For Rent" section greatly exceeds the weekday paper for two reasons:
— Sunday papers have a larger circulation than daily papers.
— Sundays, people apparently have more time to peruse ads.

Sunday classified rates are usually more expensive than daily rates.

Many landlords claim that Sunday ads are wasted. A small ad is lost in the large Sunday classified sections. Some landlords get better results with weekday ads.

Prospective tenants can distinguish between rental office ads and private owner ads. Prospective tenants assume rental offices are closed Sunday, and won't call them. On the other hand, they *will* call private owners. If the Sunday classified section is delivered on Saturday, expect calls Saturday as well.

If you will be away from home, list another number of a person who will be home. You cannot afford to miss calls. Many people still refuse to leave messages on answering machines, and some people are not calling from their own phones and can't leave a number.

Newspaper renting terms

People like to fantasize. Aim for the heart as well as the head. Use adjectives, but do not get carried away.

Acceptable adjectives:

affordable	beautiful	brand-new
charming	convenient	cozy
delightful	deluxe	desirable
discount	elegant	luxury
modern	panoramic	peaceful
plush	pretty	premier
quiet setting	prestige	private
superior	serene	spacious

Some exaggeration is acceptable.

What the place really is:	Preferred terminology:
row house	town house
old	historic
cramped	cozy
small house	starter house
wreck	handyman special
out in the boondocks	remote setting, hideaway
overgrown backyard	rustic setting
next to supermarket	adjacent to shopping
on a main highway	bus line at your door

decaying neighborhood	established neighborhood
crazy floor plan	unique floor plan

General or specific ad copy?

There are two ways to advertise rentals. Each ad provides insight into the landlord's thinking.

General: Dale County area, three-bedroom house, yard, 765-4321.

Specific: Dale County, 1706 Bell Ct., 3 BR colonial, fenced yard, A/C, $700 mo.+ SD/ref., avail. Oct. 1, 765-4321.

The landlord in the general ad appeals to the widest possible audience in the greater Dale County vicinity. Price seems negotiable, as well as security deposit and references. The house may or may not have other desirable features, but the owner is holding them for reserve.

In a general ad, the owner does not mind discussing the house's features with inquirers. If the landlord is a good salesman, he/she can get prospective tenants to examine the house who might not have done so otherwise.

In the specific ad, the owner doesn't mind saying that the house is a colonial (even though two-story houses exclude certain people) or that the house is not immediately available. Rent is set, as well as the owner's security deposit requirement and references. The landlord feels confident listing the house address. Specific ads generate fewer, but more serious, inquiries.

> *Note:* An added benefit to listing the dwelling address is that renters will drive by themselves, and, based on the outside appearance, decide whether to pursue further action. For this reason, list a house address only if your rental unit shows well on the outside.

Owners learn to fine-tune their ads. General ads become more specific as owners tire of answering numerous calls. Specific ads become more general as owners worry about getting so few calls.

Other advertising means

Advertising should not be limited to newspapers. Tenants are also secured by index card ads on community bulletin boards of supermarkets, laundromats, churches, hospitals, and universities. Choose your advertising bulletin board carefully. An ad at a corner bar may bring a different tenant from an ad on the community bulletin board of a senior center.

Create a market

A little imagination can sometimes transform an ordinary rental into a special rental. Two examples:

Example 1: If your rental is at ground level, consider renting it to the handicapped. So little housing is available for the disabled, and, ironically, the disabled often receive guaranteed benefits which can go toward rent. To attract this group, sometimes only minimal renovation is needed. If you look around, there may even be special government or private funding.

Example 2: America is graying. By the year 2000, 22.5 percent of American households will have at least one person sixty-five years old or older. If you're renting a house or apartment, try to attract the older population. They are not as transient, and their income is usually guaranteed, especially if they receive Social Security and private pensions.

—If the washer/dryer is in the basement, consider bringing it to the first floor or to one of the upstairs bedrooms.
—Install bathroom railings (grab bars) around the tub and toilet.
—If there is a family room on the first floor and bedrooms are upstairs, consider converting the first floor room to a master bedroom.
—Install D-shaped handles on cabinets and lever handles on doors. These don't require grasping or twisting.

Stereotype pitfalls

Landlords quickly learn the pitfalls of stereotyping groups. Advice books, for example, recommend selecting retired over non-retired people. Their reasoning is that retired people are stable. However, while some retired people are stable, some are also home a lot and are demanding and picky about repairs. Noise bothers some of them, and since many are on fixed incomes, some believe that they are immune to rent increases.

Advice books recommend not renting to single males. Single males are said to be transient and prone to partying. Conversely, I have heard landlords say that if any group is most likely to undertake their own repairs, it is single males!

Advice books recommend not renting to families with children. They are right. There is little good that can be said about renting to people with children. *But don't stereotype.* There are parents who tightly control four children and who are a joy to have as tenants. Conversely, there are parents whose single child runs amok, and you wish they would move elsewhere.

> *Note*: Recent federal and state laws prohibit or restrict adult-only rentals. While you may like to exclude children, it is not always possible.

Mothering to close the deal

Deals don't just happen. People have to be massaged and coaxed to do what you want. You will find this theme repeated throughout this book concerning:
— getting the tenant/buyer of your choice to say yes
— working with banks and insurance companies
— working with contractors and repair people.

To secure the tenant of your choice, "mothering" may involve:
— transporting the prospective tenant to the rental
— special accommodation, i.e., showing the rental off-hours
— calling prospective tenants and not waiting for them to call you
— extra incentives, discounts, rent with option to buy, even paying tenant's moving expense.

Tenants, as everyone else, need "mothering." Everyone wants to be loved and appreciated.

CHAPTER 6

RENT:

WHAT LANDLORDING IS ALL ABOUT

When is rent really due?

Fortunately for landlords, the biggest tenant misconception is the universally accepted belief that rent is due in advance, at the beginning of the month.

In actuality, unless parties agree otherwise, rent is due at the end of the month. (Tenants should never be told this; that is why this book is not sold to tenants.)

Parties can agree to have rent due at the beginning of the month, which is what is almost universally done. They can also agree to have rent due at the end of every seven days, seven months, seven years, etc.

> *Note*: In blue-collar neighborhoods, weekly rent is not unusual, i.e., on Fridays when workers get paid. The disadvantage, of course, is extra bookkeeping. On the plus side, landlords get an extra four weeks' rent a year since at least four months a year have *five* Fridays. Rent increases are also more palatable, i.e., a $5 a week increase sounds better than a $20 a month increase.

Where is rent really due?

A second misconception is that tenants are obligated to mail rent to the landlord or deliver rent to the landlord's premises. Under common law, rent is due at the rented premises, and it is the landlord who is obligated to make the trek to pick up the rent.

That said, a landlord and tenant can agree to put the onus on tenant, i.e., that tenant is responsible for mailing rent to landlord, or delivering it to landlord's premises. Make sure you put this requirement in your lease or rental agreement.

How much to charge

While rent must be compatible with market conditions, it is in everyone's interest for you to charge more.

Why charge more?

—More profit for you. That's ultimately why you got into the business.

—It lessens the need for future rent increases.

—It enables you to be a better landlord, i.e., you are in a better position to give more and improve the property.

—It increases the property's sale value. Higher rents justify a higher purchase price.

How are "market conditions" determined?

— what other landlords charge for comparable rentals. Newspaper ads have this information.

— tenants. Tenants let you know whether rent is acceptable.

— hit or miss. If property does not rent at one price, try another.

Rent control

New landlords often worry about rent control. The good news about rent control is that only a few areas in the country have it. And with good reason. Rental units in those areas are scarce, and without rent control, tenants would be driven out of their dwellings. Landlords in those areas operate with near 100 percent occupancy and have otherwise learned rent control loopholes.

The rest of the country has a glut of apartments in the higher and mid-price range. Rent control is not needed because supply and demand forces regulate rental rates, as indeed they should.

Discounts

My parents' generation remembers the days when apartments were scarce and building superintendents (supers) were given money "under the table" to secure occupancy.

Check newspaper ads and you will see what has happened because of a glut of rental units in the upper- and mid-priced range. (In my area, "mid-priced" is $600-$1,200 a month.) Landlords are offering discounts and enticements.

Let's look at three different concessions appearing in recent classified rental ads.

Good: $300 off first month's rent.

Better: $300 move-in allowance.

Best: Thirty-day living guarantee. Live in your new apartment for thirty days. If you are not completely satisfied, we will refund your security deposit and application fee!

The second example is better than the first because it does not discount rent. Rent remains the same, and it appears that the landlord is giving $300 out of his own pocket for a "move-in allowance."

I like the third example best for two reasons. First, because landlord gets his full month's rent. Landlords should not be in the rent discounting business. Second, because the landlord addresses a different tenant fear: "What if I'm not happy?"

If tenants are not happy, you don't want them in your property. You are returning a security deposit which you would have to return anyway. In actual practice tenants do not move after thirty days.

Other rental enticements

One of my favorites is a tenant challenge.

24-Hour Maintenance Guarantee: We promise to respond to your maintenance concerns within 24 hours or your rent is free until your problem is resolved.

The ad sounds great! It doesn't guarantee landlord will *fix* the problem within twenty-four hours, only that landlord will *respond* to tenant's maintenance concern within twenty-four hours and *resolve* the problem. Does "resolve" mean "fix"? Perhaps. To landlord, "resolve" may just mean turning the repair order over to the management company.

Rent for services

Tenants often ask for rent reductions in exchange for services. These services include collecting rent from others, showing empty apartments, snow removal where it is landlord's responsibility, etc.

Sometimes, new landlords have no choice, especially when the prior landlord approved a rent concession. The better practice is to pay tenant for his service and *not* grant rent concessions.

Why "rent for service" is not recommended
—After the first month, tenants forget the reason for the rent
    reduction. As far as they are concerned, they are performing free
    labor.
—When a landlord does not directly pay for the service, it is hard
    for a landlord to prescribe how work should be done or terminate
    further tenant service when work is unsatisfactory.
—It is hard to raise rent when a tenant is getting a rent reduction.
    Tenant can easily say, "Okay, but the price for my service is going
    up too."
—Tax implications. Strictly speaking, landlords may have to report
    as rent the fair market value of the performed services. In fact,
    when the fair market value exceeds a threshold amount, tenants
    may have to report the reduced rent as income.

Return envelopes
Did you ever wonder why credit card companies enclose return
envelopes? The reason is obvious; it facilitates and assures payments
made and delivered to the correct address. Charities go a step further
and place stamps on return envelopes. It plays on your guilt and
removes an excuse that you couldn't find a stamp.

Prudent landlords do the same. Some landlords give tenants a stack
of pre-addressed envelopes. Tenants often misplace the envelopes. A
better practice is to send the tenant a receipt around the twentieth of
the month for the prior month's rent. With the receipt, enclose a
return envelope. You are not just sending a receipt, you are sending a
reminder, and for goodwill on the return envelope, you have even
attached a stamp.

Post-dated checks
Some landlords require twelve post-dated checks at the beginning of
a tenancy. On the first of the month, the landlord has the rent in hand,
and it is tenant's responsibility to make funds available to cover the
check. Is this legal? Yes, unless prohibited by law. Landlords should
obviously explain why this policy is in tenant's best interest, i.e., time
and postage savings and peace of mind that rent has been received.

Should you let tenants make payments at your house?

Majority opinion goes against allowing tenants in your house— ever. If your house is fixed up, tenants will want the same for their rental. Some landlords rightfully fear unknown or jealous strangers entering their house.

Brave souls allow tenants to make payments at the landlord's house. When tenants pay in person, mail delay is avoided and landlord is spared from having to go to the tenant. Sharing a cup of coffee with a tenant and building goodwill goes a long way. Hospitality might encourage tenants to make repairs or improvements the landlord is otherwise responsible for.

Legal implications of accepting partial rent or security deposit

Rent is paid in advance and so is a security deposit. But there is a major difference between rent and security deposits. You can evict tenants for failure to pay rent. Most jurisdictions will not allow you to evict tenants for an unpaid security deposit.

What if a prospective tenant has only $500 for the month's rent and promises to pay the $500 security deposit over a period of months? If you have decided to accept this tenant, the better practice is to accept the $500 as a security deposit, with the month's rent paid over a few months. This way, if rent is not paid on schedule, eviction can follow.

A word of caution must be made concerning accepting partial rent.

Example: Suppose $500 a month rent due on the first is not paid. By the fifth of the month, landlord goes to court to begin eviction proceedings, and trial is set for the twentieth. Before trial on the twentieth, tenant offers landlord $250 and promises to pay the balance plus late charges in a few days. Landlords are tempted to take the $250 partial rent payment; after all, it is money in hand.

Beware. Landlords who accept partial payment may have problems enforcing a court eviction because the $500 claimed due is no longer due, rather $250 is now due and the court papers say $500! If that sounds crazy to you, imagine the surprise of landlords who have had cases thrown out of court because they accepted partial payment.

Before accepting partial payment, call the local court to see if acceptance affects eviction and if there is another way to accept partial payment without jeopardizing the pending court case.

Other security deposit considerations

In general, landlords who accept less than a month's security deposit and a month's advance rent are looking for trouble.

That said, landlords should recognize that tenants sometimes have their existing security deposits tied up with their current dwelling. For first-time tenants, besides rent and security deposit, there also is a security deposit required by the gas and electric company and another deposit required by the phone company. And too, there are tenants' moving expenses.

Tough landlords make no exceptions. Just as utility companies make no exceptions, why should landlords? Tough landlords say they would rather keep a place empty than have it occupied by tenants who do not have a month's security deposit and a month's advance rent.

Of course there is no definite answer. There are landlords who have regretted trying to work with tenants, and there are landlords whose patience has been rewarded by tenants who have honored their commitments.

The tenant bait set-up

Landlords should vigilantly guard against *tenant bait*. Some tenants have perfected this to a science.

Example: If rent is due on the first of the month, the tenant acting quite responsibly calls with a believable excuse asking if rent can be paid on the third or fourth of the month. Excuses for not having the money are ordinary.
—My car broke down and needs repairs.
—I had to send my mother an airline ticket.
—I had to outfit my child for school.

Then comes the *bait*, which is the *good* news.
—But I expect my tax refund any day.
—But my wife, girlfriend, etc. gets her commission/bonus check this week.
—But I expect my unemployment check any day now.

If you agree to the delay, what the tenant has successfully done is to shift *his* burden to *you*. You are now a partner with the promise. Several days go by, and you haven't gotten the rent. The tenant now

tells you:
  —The refund still hasn't arrived, but he checked with the IRS and the refund check is expected any day.
  —My wife's company has just decided to pay commission checks bi-monthly instead of monthly.
  —I can't believe it. I was turned down for unemployment insurance!

Any landlord claiming never to have fallen for tenant bait is either lying or the meanest son-of-a-gun who would put his invalid mother out on the street.

Short of being absolutely hard-nosed (experts say you should be) and sending eviction notices on the second of the month, even if Mother Teresa calls on the tenant's behalf, there is another approach to follow.

Hard-nosed with moderation
Here you shift the burden back to tenant. You say, "Fine, I will wait till the fourth. But in this stamped, addressed envelope I have eviction papers prepared for mailing on the fourth."

When the fourth comes without rent, you can be hard-nosed. You have already been a nice guy. There are various alternate scenarios, but at some point you're going to have to stand your ground. It might as well be early.

Should rent be due on the first of the month?
Advice books recommend that rent be due on the first of the month. If a tenant takes possession mid-month, rent is pro-rated for the balance of the month, and the next month's rent also is paid in advance.

The reason for this advice is two-fold. First, it gives landlord a chance to collect more than a month's advance rent, i.e. advance rent is collected for the pro-rated month *and* the coming month. Second, bookkeeping is easier when all rents are due on the same day.

However, if as landlord you only plan to have one or two rental units, mid-month rents are not an unbearable bookkeeping burden. Moreover, tenants sometimes prefer mid-month due dates because they obtain their funds mid-month. Not to accommodate their needs can have you and tenants feuding each month over rent due one date, but given to you on a different date.

Note: As rents approach $1,000+, in certain areas, some land-
lords now accept payments of half month's rent on the first of
the month and the other half on the fifteenth. While this is not
recommended, life's reality has made this necessary.

Should you offer incentives for on-time rent?
To assure rents are timely paid, landlords sometimes employ two
gimmicks.

Incentive 1: Landlords allow tenants to deduct $10 for rents paid on
or before the date due, i.e., rent is $600 a month; $590 if paid on or
before the first of the month.

Incentive 2: At Christmas time, landlords send $25 Christmas gift
certificates to tenants with up-to-date rents. This also kills two
proverbial birds with one stone (holiday gift and rent reward).

Purists argue that rebates should not be paid since tenants are only
doing what they are bound to do. Landlords who give rebates send tenants mixed messages, i.e., that tenants are expected to normally be late.
On the other hand, this is a less than perfect world. Some tenants are
normally late and are guided by incentives which reward behavior.
Landlords are not only teachers charged with training tenants but also
are working to improve the "bottom line." (Realize of course that
incentive #1 costs landlord $120 a year, while incentive #2 costs sub-
stantially less and may be more appreciated.)

Should you charge late fees?
Your lease should contain late fee provisions. After all, if you are late
on *your* payments you face late charges. It is tempting to forgive tenant
tardiness and waive late fees. You might be in a better financial situation than tenants. There is a certain relief when you get the rent, even
if it is late, that you are willing to forgive late charges.
Most landlords caution against ever waiving late fees. They urge
landlords never to appear soft or tenants will try to get away with just
about anything.
Tenants must know that lateness is going to cost them. Tenants must
be trained. Going easy on tenants actually makes it harder on tenants.
If you let rent due the first slide to the fifteenth of the month, tenants

will not be able to come up with the next month's rent due on the first. They will forever be in arrears.

When it gets down to it, collecting rent is the most important part of landlording, and it is the area where you have to be most vigilant. You can overlook many tenant transgressions but not pertaining to rent.

On the other hand, landlords want to be "nice guys." Landlords are also human beings who must be able to distinguish between legitimate and non-legitimate excuses. Tenants are sometimes late because they don't have the rent, and if they don't have the rent, they certainly don't have additional money for late fees.

The bottom line is that the month's rent is paid. Rules can have exceptions, and landlords have to provide a certain amount of flexibility. But make waiving late fees your *exception*, not your general "nice guy" rule.

> *Note*: If your lease provides for late fees and you waive late fees on more than one occasion, tenants may argue that late fees no longer apply. As discussed in chapter four, make sure the lease contains provisions that any waiving of landlord's rights shall not be construed as a relinquishment of those rights. If it is not in the lease, put it in writing when accepting the late payment.

Lending tenants money

Experts unanimously agree that landlords should never lend tenants money. (Believe me, tenants *will* ask.) It is neither businesslike nor professional. Dentists do not lend patients money, nor do barbers.

Charity is different. I have seen the toughest landlords place bags of food and clothes anonymously at a tenant's door.

But the issue goes deeper. The real question concerns landlord-tenant friendship. How chummy should landlord and tenant be? Most experts advise against chumminess.

Some landlords disagree and encourage tenant friendships. In some friendships, money is lent; in others the subject is taboo. They would dispute anyone advising what friends should and should not do. In keeping with this book's theme, if the practice works for you, continue what you are doing.

Failure to pay rent

Eviction. Tenants who fail to pay rent get evicted. The term is harsh and evokes images of tenants sitting curbside with their possessions.

Landlords are usually nice guys and cringe at the thought of evicting anyone. To ease your mind, use this analogy. Just as supermarkets do not let people without money leave with shopping carts full of groceries, why should landlords? Since a month's rent exceeds a basketful of groceries, the analogy is quite apt.

Some jurisdictions allow court proceedings to be initiated the day after rent is due; other jurisdictions require that tenants be given a three-day notice to pay rent or quit the premises. In either situation, there is no excuse for not serving notice immediately.

> *Note*: Tenants defaulting on rent are usually in default of other lease provisions. These often do not require a three-day notice, and landlords can seek immediate eviction.

Must landlords accept late rent?

Generally, the answer is yes. Late rent also can include late charges and court fees. However, many jurisdictions recognize the landlord's burden of having to continuously sue for rent and allow landlords to refuse late-tendered rent after the third or fourth time.

Rent abatement

Tenants in default of rent usually come up with all sorts of excuses, the most common being that repairs have not been made. Minor defects become major complaints. Judges see these tactics used all the time, and they are not always as sympathetic to tenants as landlords fear, i.e. not all repairs justify tenants withholding rent.

Nonetheless, courts will order the landlord to make necessary repairs. When landlords are "repeat offenders," courts may order rent paid to the court in escrow. In extreme cases, or when defects are substantial, courts may order a rent reduction, i.e., reduce the $600 monthly rent to $400 for the period the house lacked heat. (I heard one yuppie argue to be excused from rent because he could not entertain as he would have liked on his defective patio deck. While the court ordered the landlord to fix the deck, rent and late charges had to be paid.)

Utilities

When a tenant fails to pay rent, it is mighty tempting to think about turning off the tenant's utilities. This is illegal in many jurisdictions, and landlords cannot otherwise cut off water, gas, heat, electricity, etc. Some jurisdictions even categorize this as *criminal*.

Eviction

Courts allow the tenant a last opportunity to pay rent, and when the second opportunity passes, courts allow landlords to schedule eviction. Some jurisdictions actually let landlords put tenants' possessions on the street; others require landlords to store tenant's possessions at landlord's expense. Some jurisdictions allow sheriffs to seize tenants' possessions for sale to pay back rent.

In actual practice, tenants and their possessions are usually out of the dwelling when the sheriff, marshal, or constable arrives.

> *Note*: It is easier to evict tenants during certain months than in others. Many areas cancel evictions on rain or snow days or if freezing conditions are predicted. Landlords must arrange for new eviction dates.

Public assistance

There are times when landlords can provide alternative help. Distressed tenants may not know that they qualify for certain assistance. Sometimes, they lack basic transportation to get them to offices where assistance is processed. Landlords are not obligated to help tenants in this fashion, but if it helps secure rent or helps tenants find different housing, assistance is to your advantage.

Some tenants look for eviction. That may sound extreme, but in some areas, tenants who face eviction receive emergency public assistance. They need eviction papers to receive assistance. Some tenants do this on a regular basis. I am not advocating landlord fraud, i.e., cooperating with tenants falsely claiming poverty. But on the other hand, when a tenant fails to pay rent, the landlord is not obligated to conduct an investigation into why the tenant has no funds.

Pursuing deadbeats

I don't usually pursue deadbeats. To me it is a waste of energy that produces a grumpy landlord. Landlording is supposed to be fun; lost rent is just another cost of doing business. As a landlord, all I want is my house back in reasonably good shape.

Lawsuits involve time away from work and legal costs. It is rare when lawsuits don't produce counter suits. A favorable judgment is not a victory if landlord is unable to collect, as often happens. As a landlord, I can make better use of my time negotiating better insurance coverage, bank financing, or more carefully selecting my tenants.

Going for the jugular

Some landlords are not content to just get their dwelling back in reasonable shape after a tenant leaves owing money. Some landlords pursue tenants for every dollar owed.

Some landlords claim it is a matter of principle and will go to tenant's employer, new landlord, etc. Is this recommended? Problems arise when debt collection changes from a business pursuit to a personal vendetta. Obviously, each case differs. If you can stomach this approach and the approach works for you, use it. If not, relax—you can still be a successful landlord.

> *Note*: If you do pursue this route, many lawyers handle landlord claims on a contingency basis. Also, debtor bank account locator services will locate debtor assets anywhere in the country for a flat fee (i.e., $125 a search) or on contingency. This aids getting uncollected judgments collected.

Increasing rent

Landlords fear asking tenants for rent increases the way employees fear asking bosses for a raise.

Landlords conjure up all sorts of reasons why they should not ask for a rent increase:
—The tenant will move.
—The tenant cannot afford it.
—The rent is already higher than average.
—The tenant has other personal problems.
—The tenant does his own repairs.
—The tenant will ask for all sorts of improvements.

Landlords who carefully establish high rents at the beginning of the tenancy do not have to raise rents as often as other landlords. Less ill will is created. There is a certain logic to not rocking the boat regarding rents, or, "If it ain't broke, don't fix it."

Rents should be raised for a reason, i.e., fuel, insurance, or taxes have gone up tremendously, or you made all sorts of improvements and the dwelling is now worth more, etc. Tenants understand the need for rent increases in these circumstances. You even put their minds at ease, especially if they thought the increase would be greater.

Sometimes, it pays to raise rents precisely to remove a problem tenant. Sometimes it pays to raise rents to encourage a tenant to buy your property, especially if ownership is comparable to renting. Conversely, if a tenant has made all sorts of repairs and improvements—improvements that landlords normally absorb, a rent increase might send the wrong signal.

The bottom line is that necessity forces you to raise rents. At that point, all your landlord excuses fall aside, and you develop courage to ask for a raise. To make it easier for the tenant, tell him/her that the increase will go in effect two months down the road.

CHAPTER 7

HOUSE COMPONENTS:

FROM A LANDLORD'S PERSPECTIVE

There are two types of houses: *owner-occupied* and *rental*. The biggest mistake new landlords make is confusing the two. Repairs and improvements a landlord makes on his own house are not necessarily wise for rental property.

House front
Curb appeal is more important for rental property than private residential property. It has been said that houses are rented or rejected before tenants walk through the door.

If a landlord on a tight budget has to choose between fixing the outside or the inside, most professionals would fix the outside.

The exterior should not look like it needs painting. Street-facing windows should be in good shape. If you install storm windows, at least install them on street-facing windows.

If there is a lawn, it must be neat, not overgrown. A few perennial plants do wonders. Suggested plants are azaleas in sunny spots and rhododendrons in shady spots. These plants are generally maintenance-free and make the house attractive, especially when in bloom. Spring bulbs and certain tulips planted once give years of joy. Evergreens are inexpensive and look good year-round.

Plants and shrubs are nice gifts to give tenants, especially since tenants do not normally buy these items. You use tenant labor to put your plants into the ground. It improves your property while the tenant has satisfaction watching the plants grow.

> *Note:* Don't assume tenants have shovels and trowels for planting; you may have to loan these items.

In the spring, consider giving tomato plants for the backyard. It's almost a guarantee tenants will stay till summer's end to reap the fruits. (For that reason, don't give early ripening hybrids.)

Windows should not be bare; at least install shades. Bare windows proclaim a house's emptiness. This is something potential vandals do not need to know. Shades provide a lived-in look, and window coverings are one less item tenants have to worry about immediately after moving in. If your interior windows aren't in the best condition, shades also direct attention *away* from the windows.

> *Comment:* Landlords must learn on a case by case basis to distinguish between *deception* and *illusion*. Everything today involves marketing, and part of marketing is illusion. If shades direct attention away from windows that are not in the best shape, so be it. That is *illusion*. Nevertheless, no one likes *deception*.

Window shutters, whether plastic or wood, also add charm to a house. Moreover, they add value to the house when you sell.

Door and window awnings also are appreciated and add tremendous resale value.

Exterior improvements need not be expensive. Non-costly items include:

— awnings
— brass house numbers
— brass kickplate
— brass mail slot
— brass door knocker
— decorative bell
— decorative mailbox
— freshly painted door
— freshly painted handrails
— freshly painted picket fence
— ground level planters
— hanging plant baskets
— lawn decorations
— outdoor lights
— storm windows
— window boxes
— window shutters.

Note: Exterior improvements are like jewelry. There must be moderation. Do not embellish the house with every single item listed above or your house will look like an advertisement for a hardware store!

House numbers

It's surprising how many houses lack identifying house numbers. Nothing frustrates potential tenants and later guests more than not being able to find the house.

For under $25, landlords can distinctively outfit a house with house numbers that immediately set the tone the landlord is trying to convey.

Bell

If there is a front bell, see that it works, or remove it. Most housing codes do not require working front doorbells, but a non-working bell is one of the first things a tenant sees and it indicates the condition of the rest of the house. Once the tenant moves in the house, a non-working bell is a continuing source of irritation, especially when it has to be explained to every guest.

Railings

If local housing codes do not require front step railings, (this is based on the height of the door from the ground), the cautious landlord should hesitate before installing railings. That sounds crass; however, once railings are installed, landlords are charged with maintenance. Tenants and their guests are not as careful with railings as homeowners, and the situation is exasperated when tenants have small children.

Note: When insurance companies require railings, you do not have this leeway.

Steps

In some areas, homeowners paint their front concrete steps. Landlords should always strive to keep their properties maintenance-free, including steps. Unless you enjoy step painting, go for the natural look. If the steps are painted, apply a fresh coat of paint between vacancies. It is part of curb appeal and first impression.

Brick exteriors

Some homeowners paint brick exteriors. Landlords who paint brick exteriors are looking for added maintenance expenses. Avoid the temptation of planting ivy. Ivy quickly overgrows. Roots get into the cement joining the bricks and may get into windows.

Doors

Doors are part of curb appeal. If there is any room in your budget for frill, a decorative front door is a great investment. Most people have never had to buy a door. New landlords find that there are two types of doors: hollow-core doors for interior use and solid-core doors for exterior use. Doors in multi-unit dwellings also may have to meet certain fire codes.

Doors should be secure. Every now and then, newspapers report cases going in tenants' favor where landlords were liable for intruders gaining entry through improperly secured doors. Liability aside, secure, attractive doors pay for themselves.

Door locks

If you plan to own a number of buildings, consider having cylinders keyed to a master key. It's a one-time expense. Otherwise, you will walk around with a jail warden's ring of keys. It also makes life easier for any management company you use.

A landlord I know has one master key for his hundred units but uses only three different cylinders for tenants. Keys are labeled, "A," "B," and "C." As landlord, he cuts only three sets of keys. He keeps a large supply of each set and does not have to run to the hardware store every time a cylinder is changed. When tenants move, he changes an "A" cylinder for a "B" cylinder, etc.

Even if you don't do your own plumbing and electrical work, changing cylinders is an easy skill to learn. Tenants feel better knowing former tenants do not have their entry key. As landlord, you make your life easier. Since you are changing cylinders, you do not have to track down previously issued keys.

Same for padlocks. If padlocks are going to go on various basement doors, sheds, etc., you may as well purchase a number of locks with the same key code. One key for all padlocks makes a landlord's life much easier.

Note: Before you saw off an unknown padlock, bring the serial number to your local locksmith. Locksmiths can sometimes duplicate keys using serial numbers.

Ceiling fans

Front room ceiling fans make tremendous first impressions. A ceiling fan and light kit can be obtained almost as inexpensively as a lighting fixture. When selling a house, ceiling fans, strategically placed, boost the house selling price.

Whether to use expensive fixtures depends on the property. When rent is higher, more is expected.

Skylights

Skylights in rental properties are improvements that more than pay for themselves in rents, ease of renting, and resale.

If a room has a skylight, tenants or buyers may overlook other defects. People actually fall in love with sky-lit rooms. Skylights fulfill tenant fantasies.

Tenant fantasies

Unless you deal with luxury dwellings, tenants are often people of limited means. They may be newlyweds, students, widowed, single parents, newly divorced, recent immigrants, military people, etc.

Some experts characterize tenants as "non-imaginative" people who can acquire life's comforts only by renting. Such people could probably never afford to rent or purchase magazine-type houses that normally come with skylights and other lavish, glitzy items. This is the psychology employed by hotels with heart-shaped beds and other extravagances.

Rental properties do not generally include lavish amenities. When installed in your property, amenities sell the dwelling and your vacancy period is shorter.

The time to install skylights is not when your ceiling and roof is in perfect condition. But consider it when making ceiling or roof repairs.

Decks

A deck is another frill that more than pays for itself. As a general rule, an item is worth installing if it is an item that you would put in a newspaper advertisement listing your property for rent or sale.

Example: For Rent, 3BR Townhouse, deck, 765-4321.

Porches

Experts recommend *against* purchasing a house with a porch. If a house has a porch, they recommend ripping it out. Their reason: too many potential problems. Porches are usually wooden appendages to houses. Steps become bad, floors begin to sag, and porch roofs, poorly constructed to begin with, leak.

This advice makes certain sense. If the house you are buying is destined only for rental, you do not need a porch as a potential liability. On the other hand, if you have hopes of a later home-owner sale, a porch is a valuable asset giving new owners hours of joy and use.

Fireplace

Americans are fondly attached to fireplaces which conjure up images of warmth and family. If your rental house has a working fireplace, be sure to clean the flue every so often. You can be sure tenants will not do this. When renting or selling, place a few logs on the fireplace to accent this feature.

For houses and apartments without fireplaces, consider installing mantlepieces. Again, it is part of tenant fantasy. A working or even non-working fireplace can make the difference between rental or vacancy.

Other luxury items

New landlords eager to attract quality tenants often install high-priced luxury items such as a:
— washer/dryer
— dishwasher
— self-cleaning oven.

There should be one consideration before providing these items: *cost of capital*.

If it costs $2,500 to install a washer/dryer, dishwasher, and self-cleaning oven lasting ten years, the landlord must recoup through extra rent:
— the interest (approximately $25 a month for these three items)
— $250 a year straight line-depreciation (approximately $20 a month. After ten years, these items have to be replaced.)

— repair costs or appliance repair contracts (approximately $15 a month).

In this scenario, if these appliances generate an additional $60 a month in rents, the $2,500 installation expense may be justified. If they don't generate $60 a month in additional rents, installation may be a non-reimbursable frill.

> *Note:* Some landlords engrave their driver's license number on expensive, removable items such as furnaces, washing machines, etc. This helps police track stolen objects. Some police departments even provide landlords with special stickers to be placed in unseen areas. (Driver's license numbers are used, not social security numbers, because while the former is public record, the latter is not.)

Central air-conditioning
The good news about installing central air-conditioning is that it is not as expensive as you think, especially if the house has heat ducts. But the same cost of capital consideration applies. If installation is $2,500, will it generate an additional $60 a month (as found above) to cover depreciation, interest, and repairs?

There is another air-conditioning consideration. Can the tenant afford its operation? If the tenant can barely afford normal monthly rent and utilities (as you will too often find), will the tenant's budget be exhausted by the extra $100 a month spent for air-conditioning between May and October? If your rental unit is in a low-income area, caution is advised before installing an energy-eating luxury item.

Painting
If you paint, pick harmless colors. While your favorite color may be lavender or orange, this may repulse prospective tenants. White is the preferred apartment color, but houses are more individual and can tolerate more color. Daring color is suggested, especially to brighten the appearance of drab, dingy spaces.

One inexpensive device landlords use to improve appearance is to use different colors to highlight house details. On the outside, doors and windows are painted one color, walls another, and ornamentation a third. On interior walls, inexpensive molding separates the bottom half painted one color and the top portion painted another color.

Paint bargains

Don't be afraid of paint bargains. Bargains may include paint mixed for a buyer who ultimately chose a different color. A frugal landlord buys a gallon of such paint and softens it with a few gallons of inexpensive white paint.

> *Note*: While you should try to get a landlord's or contractor's discount on all house purchases, paint discounts are among the easiest to obtain. *But you have to ask.* You may be required to show certain proof that you own investment property.

If you expect to buy paint frequently, locate paint stores specializing in *closeouts*. These include discontinued colors and paints with minor defects.

If you expect to paint after every tenant, it makes no sense to buy premium ten-year paint when tenants are only expected to stay a year or two. Professional management companies generally apply fresh coats of the cheapest white paint after each tenant. A clean, new look is obtained at minimal cost.

> *Note*: Some landlords buy only a single color, i.e., white, in large multi-gallon containers. Landlords never have problems matching colors, and it is easy to give tenants small jars of touch-up paint.

Flat paint vs. semi-gloss

Flat paint is cheaper than semi-gloss and applies more easily to walls. Flat paint discharges beautifully out of paint spray guns. Who uses flat paint? Landlords who plan to paint after each tenant. Other landlords use semi-gloss paint which is easier to wash clean and saves the landlord from having to repaint after each tenant.

Latex vs. oil paint

While you might use oil-based paint for your own house (presumably because it lasts longer), never do so on tenant property. Painters using oil paints charge more because oil is harder to apply and clean-up is more complicated. Even with the lid tightly on, oil paints harden when stored in cans. Once oil paint is applied to a wall, you almost always have to continue using oil because latex does not adhere to oil-based surfaces.

Tenants are not looking for long-lasting paint applications; they want clean, freshly painted walls. If the average homeowner moves once every seven years, the average tenant moves even more frequently. Thus, it makes no sense to apply long-lasting oil paint. Too, it is a cardinal rule of landlording that whatever existing color is on the wall, the tenant despises the color and it will have to be redone. So stay away from oil.

> *Note*: Never mix oil-based paint with latex paint or outdoor-use paints with indoor-use paints. It doesn't go.

Wallpaper

Do not wallpaper rental property. Again, the cardinal rule applies. Whatever is up, the tenant won't like. Removing wallpaper is messy and expensive.

Wallpaper has its place where it is the cheapest material to cover defective walls. However, there is no reason to use first-quality rolls when wallpaper stores practically give away wallpaper with "blems" or slightly imperfect patterns.

To make small rooms look larger, decorating books advise mural-pattern wallpaper. They caution against choosing patterns with large solid colors which make rooms look smaller.

Floors

Sometimes the cheapest way to improve the appearance of deteriorated wood floors is simply to apply a coat of fresh paint. This holds true in rooms such as upstairs bedrooms which are not seen on first impression, and will probably have some other tenant floor covering, i.e., area rug. In these instances, the best floor paint is outdoor deck paint. Use a neutral, non-offensive color, or brown to simulate the color of wood floors.

> *Note*: Consider applying a polyurethane coat to the painted floor for extra shine and durability.

A second flooring option is either laid linoleum or stick-in-place tile.

Per square foot, linoleum is usually cheaper; however, if holes develop, the entire piece needs replacement.

Stick-on-tiles can be installed by almost anyone, with one caveat. The sub-flooring must be good. While it is possible to find quarter-inch plywood, thicker plywood is preferred. (Caution: When using thicker plywood, make sure you have clearance for doors.)

Pressed particle-board is sufficient for most rooms, provided they are not rooms where water hits the floors, such as bathrooms and kitchens. When particle-board gets wet, it warps, ruining the tile or linoleum above it.

Carpeting

Carpeting is more practical and economical than you think. Some landlords prefer carpeting because it hides floor defects, is a one-time investment, cleans reasonably well, and has a prescribed life span.

Decorators claim wall-to-wall carpeting makes rooms look larger. Decorators caution against using either dark or light colors which show dirt. They recommend using variegated and pepper-and-salt patterns. For a decorator-look, if you get hold of an inexpensive area rug or small piece of carpeting, consider painting the floor *around* the rug.

> Note: Scores of household tips abound for removing carpet stains. A favorite for removing carpet furniture dents is simply to allow ice cubes to melt in the depression and swell the fibers back to normalcy.

Since carpeting is being installed for tenant use, you may wish to look at carpet store or carpet factory's "seconds" or odd-lot pieces.

For low-income housing, you may wish to get *used* carpeting. Carpet installers sometimes throw away almost perfectly good carpeting for various reasons. Sometimes, existing carpeting does not go with the customer's new furniture, or customers want to rip up carpeting to install wood floors. Used carpeting is perfectly good, and the price is certainly right. If you feel guilty, install new padding. It gives carpeting whole new life.

Where you have carpeting, it is not a bad policy to professionally clean the carpets between tenants. Carpet-cleaning services do fairly decent work.

Note: When using a carpet service, where feasible ask for the service that is mounted to the truck and which has extra cleaning power (not the hand-held equipment).

Paneling and ceiling tiles

Except for basements, most people consider paneling and ceiling tiles "tacky." Landlords view paneling differently. Paneling and ceiling tiles do not show signs of age and generally last through many years of tenants. It is a low-cost way to cover defective walls, and for ceilings, there is no better way to cover ceiling defects than with inexpensive two-by-four-foot ceiling tiles.

An idea many landlords use is to install paneling in half four-by-four-foot sections for the bottom half of the wall, and to plaster the upper half of the wall. The advantage is that the upper wall can hold tenants' pictures, and holes driven into the walls can easily be spackled. A paint job requires only half the work and is something amateurs can tackle.

Note: For spackling holes in walls, a "Heloise" type tip is to fill the hole with toothpaste and wipe the spot with a wet cloth or sponge. The result is less noticeable than trying to match the wall color with touch-up paint.

Paneling ranges in price from a few dollars a sheet to the high teens. There is attractive waterproof paneling designed for kitchens and bathrooms which can save the expense of tiling.

Note: Landlords quickly learn that you can't just purchase four-by-eight-foot paneling and tie it to the car top. It is too large and too brittle. It does not fit into a regular station wagon, and if you tie it to the top, you're looking for trouble. Trust me, I have learned through bitter experience that the only way to successfully transport paneling is with a van or have it delivered.

Windows

When replacing panes, use acrylic; it is safer and does not need replacement. Some landlords purposely do not install window guards. While tenants with small children benefit from window guards, a legal nightmare can ensue if, during a fire, a tenant's exit is hampered or the window guard proves defective.

For the same reason, some landlords do *not* install window screens. While screens are not meant to be window guards, tenants have brought lawsuits where children fell through screens.

Baseboard electric heat

Some landlords install electric baseboard heat because it is cheaper than installing a heating system requiring a furnace and duct work. This makes sense in areas where electric rates are low or where heat is rarely used.

In northern areas, electric baseboard heat for tenants is financially catastrophic. Tenants moving in the summer may be indifferent to the type of heat, but when that first electric heat bill comes, you will hear about it. They will probably move or plan to be out of your dwelling the following year.

> *Note*: Be alert to municipal weatherization programs. Your tenants may be eligible for energy audits and weatherization assistance. This can include overhauling the house's heating system, storm windows, caulking, etc.

Stoves

Landlords paying for utilities should definitely consider replacing existing pilot-lit stoves with *pilotless ignition stoves*. On stoves using natural gas, pilotless ignition saves up to a third of the energy consumed by pilot-lit stoves. If you plan to keep the house a while and/or energy costs are high, the savings are significant. Note, however, repair costs are higher for stoves with electronic ignitions, and the electronic ignition is one more item for tenants to break.

Closets

Renters especially desire closets for the simple reason that they often have not yet accumulated furniture. Even if you merely provide space, closets are one item tenants will improve themselves. Tenants are often creative and proud of their work. They usually leave closet improvements for the next tenant.

Smoke detectors

Smoke detectors are relatively inexpensive and provide a smart look when showing a house or apartment. They pay for themselves when insurance companies give discounts for smoke-detector-equipped houses. However before rushing to install them, see if you are responsible to install them, and what type.

While most jurisdictions require smoke detectors for houses and apartments where landlords rent more than four units in a building, the obligation may be the tenant's. Some jurisdictions require smoke detectors attached to an electrical source with a battery backup. Local laws vary on installation responsibility in multiple-family units. You may wish to check with your local fire department.

The reason to verify responsibility is because, if the smoke detector proves faulty or has not been installed properly, the landlord is blamed. Malfunctioning or improperly installed units can otherwise give tenants a false sense of security.

The same holds true for fire extinguishers and burglar alarms. If the landlord is not responsible to provide it, *don't*.

> *Note:* Nice gifts to give tenants are smoke detectors, fire extinguishers, and detachable burglar alarms. But they must be *gifts* which tenants can take when they move. If the units malfunction or are improperly installed, it will not be the landlord's fault. Be sure, if you are worried about liability, to remove these items when the tenant leaves; they are easily overlooked.

Meters: Gas, electric, water

Utility companies install meters, and not much can be said about meters. But meters can err! This is critical when landlords pay for utilities.

Of late, a whole new profession has arisen—*utility auditors*. Utility auditors work on commission, i.e., 50 percent of what they recoup or save the client for two to five years. Utility auditors check for uncalibrated meters. They check for computer and human errors. They compare clients' bills against utility company tariff rates.

Roofs

Tenants occasionally use the roof for personal use. Use might include sunbathing, hanging clothes, or even installing a hot tub.

Besides damage to roofs built only to accommodate the natural elements, liability insurance may or may not cover roof-area accidents.

Courts ruling on these matters have generally ruled in the landlord's favor, i.e., that roofs are meant to only shelter tenants. Roof use by tenants is not included in the basic lease.

Furnished or unfurnished

Consider furnishing a rental unit if you have an accumulated source of excess furniture. There are pros and cons to renting a furnished dwelling.

Advantages to renting furnished dwellings

—Furnished dwellings command more rent. Some landlords recover the furniture cost in just a short period of time.

—There are many reasons why people want furnished dwellings, especially today when people constantly move and life situations change so rapidly. Furnished dwellings are no longer reserved for skid-row bums.

—Furniture depreciation provides a nice tax savings. Furnishing an apartment gives you something to do with inherited furniture that is too good to give away but not needed in your personal dwelling.

—Your newspaper ad gets extra attention. See how few furnished dwelling ads there are. As a rule, landlords are still scared of providing a furnished premises. If you have never tried it, you will never know if it is good for you.

Disadvantages to renting furnished dwellings

—Landlords renting furnished dwellings limit their prospects to only a small population.

—Tenants abuse furniture and walk off with things. (While hotel managers and innkeepers can relate horror stories, as a rule, guest abuse can't be too bad or hotels and inns would be out of business.)

—Tenants renting furnished dwellings are more transient. (While this may be true, even transient tenants sometimes stay longer than expected. In some situations, landlords can better accommodate "revolving-door" tenants, i.e., since furniture doesn't move in and out, there is less "down-time" between tenants.)

—Landlords renting furnished dwellings can have situations where tenants pick and choose what pieces of furniture they want and what they want removed. Landlords don't always have the storage space or manpower to accommodate such requests.

HOUSE CHECKLIST

DATE_____

PROPERTY _____

I. *Front Appearance*

Sidewalk:	OK ___	Lawn:	OK ___
Front steps:	OK ___	Railing:	OK ___
Porch:	OK ___	House numbers:	OK ___
Gutters:	OK ___	Front windows:	OK ___
Storm windows:	OK ___	Sills/frames need painting:	___
Broken or loose:	___	Storm door:	OK ___
Door screens:	OK ___	Front door:	OK ___
Weatherstripping required:	___	Lock:	OK ___
Front bell:	OK ___	Mailbox:	OK ___
Outdoor light:	___		

Suggested improvements:

_____

_____

_____

_____

_____

_____

_____

_____

_____

_____

II. *Basement*

Basement steps:............OK ___	Railing: ....OK ___
Floor: ......Dirt ___ Cement ___	Floor condition:..........OK ___
Damp: .... ___	Water problem:................ ___
Sump pump: .... ___	Water shut-off accessible:. ___
Copper plumbing.............. ___	Finished walls: .... ___
Finished ceiling: .... ___	Ceiling lights: ....OK ___
Basement neat: .... ___	Furnace: ....Gas ___ Oil ___

Filter last cleaned/changed: _____

Thermostat:.................OK ___   Water heater: Gas___ Elec ___

Smoke detector: ....___

Electricity: Fuse box: ___   Circuit breakers: ___   # of Amps ___
                     Wiring: ....Copper ___ ....Aluminum ___

Basement Comments:

_____

_____

_____

_____

III. *Kitchen*

Windows: Move up and down freely...............yes: ___ ......no: ___

Floor:...........................OK ___	Coming up or damaged: .. ___
Kitchen sink:................OK ___	leaks/ poor condition:...... ___
Water pressure:............OK ___	Refrigerator: ....OK ___
Stove:...........................OK ___	Dishwasher:................OK ___

Sufficient outlets:............... ___

Water spots on ceiling:....................................yes ___ .... no ___

Walls: ....OK ___   Outside kitchen door .OK ___

Comments on kitchen:

_____

_____

_____

IV. Bathroom

Door ....good condition ____

Toilet: ....good condition ____   running ____

Sink: ....good condition ____   Water pressure: ....OK ____

Towel racks: ....OK ____   Walls around tub: ....OK ____

Loose tiles: .... ____   Bathtub faucet: ....OK ____

Pressure: ....OK ____   Is tub faucet over tub level:____

Light fixture: ....OK ____

Bathroom comments

_____

_____

_____

_____

_____

V. Backyard

Back door: OK ____ Locks tight: ____ Weatherstripping needed: ____

Building foundation: OK ____   needs grading:____   caulking: ____

Backyard condition: Neat ____   Loaded with junk____

Backyard fence: OK ____   Problem ____   No fence ____

Outside wall (rear):   OK ____   Needs paint or cement: ____

Back gutters or downspouts: OK ____   Problem ____

Rear windows: OK ____   Need painting ____   Other_____

Comments on backyard:

_____

_____

_____

_____

_____

_____

VI. *Interior rooms*

Interior steps:...............OK ____

Living Room:

Floors: ....OK ____	Carpeting: ....OK ____
Walls: ....OK ____	Ceilings:.......................OK ____
Sufficient outlets:............... ____	Fireplace: ....OK ____
Windows: ....OK ____	Screens:............................ ____

Living rooms comments:

_____

_____

_____

_____

_____

_____

Dining room:

Floors: ....OK ____	Carpeting: ....OK ____
Walls: ....OK ____	Ceilings:.......................OK ____
Sufficient outlets:............... ____	Sufficient closets:.............. ____
Windows: ....OK ____	Screens:............................ ____

Dining room comments:

_____

_____

_____

_____

_____

_____

Bedroom # 1

Floors ....OK ___   Carpeting: ....OK ___

Walls: ....OK ___   Ceilings:......................OK ___

Sufficient closets:............... ___   Sufficient outlets:.............. ___

Windows: ....OK ___   Screens............................ ___

Bedroom #1 comments:

_____

_____

_____

_____

Bedroom # 2

Floors ....OK ___   Carpeting: ....OK ___

Walls: ....OK ___   Ceilings:......................OK ___

Sufficient closets:............... ___   Sufficient outlets:.............. ___

Windows: ....OK ___   Screens............................ ___

Bedroom #2 comments:

_____

_____

_____

_____

Bedroom #3

Floors ....OK ___   Carpeting: ....OK ___

Walls: ....OK ___   Ceilings:......................OK ___

Sufficient closets:............... ___   Sufficient outlets:.............. ___

Windows: ....OK ___   Screens............................ ___

Bedroom #3 comments

_____

_____

_____

_____

VII. Roof:
    Roof: Type _____
    Installed _____(year)
    Last checked _____
    Soffits:...........................OK ___

Roof comments:

_____

_____

_____

_____

VIII. Garage:
    Garage Door:................OK ___   Walls, ceiling: ....OK ___
    Interior floor: ....OK ___   Garage roof: ....OK ___
    Drain: ....OK ___

Garage comments:

_____

_____

_____

_____

CHAPTER 8

FINANCING

Preparing for loan approval—do your homework first.
Even before signing a contract for your first house, you can speed up
the bank loan application process by doing a little preliminary work.

— *Clear up judgments or outstanding balances on credit reports.*
Applications have been held up because of delinquent student
loans (even bankruptcy does not discharge these loans-you might
as well pay them) and department store balances, i.e., items that
were claimed to have been returned but which the store still
carries as "open." There may be judgments against you that were
paid but are still carried as "open." Clear these items now.

— *tax returns.* You will be asked to produce tax returns for the last
two years, especially if you are self-employed. If you do not have
a copy of your return (it is amazing how many people don't), ask
the IRS now how to get a copy. The time to get this information
is now, not while your application is pending before a bank
board.

— *balance sheet and income statement.* You will be asked to submit a
personal balance sheet and income statement, so you might as
well prepare these now. Consider in advance items you want
included and excluded as income, i.e., alimony, gifts, loans due
from others, etc. Unfortunately, you do not have this discretion
with expenses, and failing to include certain expenses may be
considered fraudulent.

— *references.* If you plan to use people as references, get their
current addresses and telephone numbers, and verify that they
will provide good references. You don't want surprises.

— *property credentials.* If you have done rehab work in your own
house or for others, prepare photographs of your work. Your

rehabbing skill is a valuable asset and also demonstrates an ability to work with funds and material. If you oversaw a rehab bing project, prepare a dossier too. Everyone loves to be part of the rehabbing process.

The loan interview

The axiom that lenders lend only to people who *don't* need money is as true today as ever.

Besides preparing your financial resume, you also must prepare for the interview. Some people even rehearse with a spouse or a friend. The loan interview process is one of balanced moderation. One must:
— be prompt for the interview, not early nor late.
— be friendly without being overbearing or pushy.
— be dressed well but not flashy.
— be poised and confident, not nervous or pompous.
— be knowledgeable without being conceited.
— be able to *ask* questions as well as answer them.

Post-interview thank-you letters are not only courteous but also allow you to confirm important points and resolve unanswered questions.

Debt-equity ratios

This phrase is important because bankers often ask for your D/E ratio. An example can best explain *debt-equity ratio.*

Example 1: Sally owes $85,000 on a $100,000 property. Sally's D/E is 85 percent debt, 15 percent equity.

Example 2: Sally owes $150,000 on a $300,000 property. Sally's D/E is 50 percent debt, 50 percent equity.

D/E also measures your financial progress.

Example: After five years of mortgage payments on an $85,000 mortgage, Sally owes $80,000 in principal. If the property is now worth $120,000, Sally's D/E is now two-thirds debt, one-third equity. Equity (ownership) interest more than doubled from *Example 1.*

Real estate debt differs from the debts of other industries. In most industries, assets rapidly depreciate in value, i.e., a bus, truck, or an airplane. Real estate asset values, however, generally rise or remain the same. They rarely decrease.

Example 1: Tom borrows $100,000 to buy a passenger bus. After five years the bus, no longer new, is worth $50,000.

Example 2: Jerry borrows $100,000 to buy a single-family house. After five years Jerry can realistically expect the house to be worth $100,000, and with appreciation, probably more.

This is why real estate debt should not be equated with the debts of other industries. As you deal with banks, you will find that too often bankers confuse business debt with real estate debt, i.e., bankers will claim that you already carry too much debt. Investors must convince lenders that real estate loans differ from regular loans and the debt they carry is not really "debt" but marketable full-value assets.

What is a good D/E to have?
Every industry sets its own D/E standards. For certain industries large debt ratios are normal, while for other industries large debts are a danger sign.

In the trucking industry, 70 percent debt, 30 percent equity is said to be acceptable. This is the ratio I strive for, although no ratio is "correct." As mentioned, real estate is one of those industries where large debt ratios can be acceptable. In fact, get-rich-from-real-estate experts recommend 100 percent debt, as will happen when you exclusively use OPM, *other people's money*. Some even recommend 110 percent debt, i.e., borrowing more than the property is worth! This might be fine for some. People I know, however, would rather sleep at night.

Secured debt vs. unsecured debt
Secured debt, as its name implies, is debt secured by collateral. The most common example of secured debt is a mortgage where bank-lent money is secured by a recorded mortgage. The most common collateral is property.

Unsecured debt is debt where there is only a *promise* to pay. Common examples are credit card bills and personal lines of credit. If borrower defaults, lender has no specific collateral.

Unsecured debt to income ratio
This is another ratio bankers use to determine financial fitness, particularly when loans are not secured by a mortgage.

Example: Carlo has $5,000 in assorted unsecured debts, $50,000 annual income, and needs $10,000 for a rehab project. Carlo's debt-income ratio is 10 percent ($50,000 income: $5,000 debt).

A financial institution that does not permit unsecured debt to exceed 25 percent will not allow Carlo's total debt to exceed $12,500 ($5,000 existing debt + $7,500 in new debt).

Bankers set debt-to-income ratios because they know that people have other obligations besides servicing debt, i.e., food, clothing, shelter, transportation, etc. Problems arise when debts exceed certain ratios. Banks want to prevent this from happening.

Every financial institution has its own criteria and definition of debt, i.e., home mortgage, investment property mortgage, student and car loans, credit card balances exceeding six months, alimony, judgments, etc. Similarly, every institution has its own criteria determining income. Some banks include projected rents as income, some banks do so only when there are leases, and some banks consider only a portion of the projected rents as income.

In the above example, Carlo will not get all the funds needed for his project because his projected debt will exceed the bank's 25 percent debt-income ratio. Carlo must convince the loan officer that the bank's debt-income ratio should not apply. Carlo will explain that borrowed funds are not being used for personal, non-income-producing items such as a vacation or new furniture, but rather will be used to generate additional income. Some banks accept this reasoning, some do not.

Types of interest
Interest can be categorized in contrasting terms:
— adjustable rate vs. fixed rate
— secured rate vs. non-secured rate
— investor rate vs. homeowner rate
— preferred customer vs. regular customer.

Adjustable vs. fixed rate

Adjustable rates, also known as variable rates, came into vogue after banks and lending institutions were caught in the mid-1970s with huge loan portfolios at low fixed rates. While the prime rate reached a high of 21 percent, banks were being repaid with low interest.

To protect themselves, some lenders require variable rates. These are set by a published prime rate, the Standard and Poor rate, U.S. Treasury notes, etc.

> *Note*: Just because your rate is variable does not mean you cannot negotiate a *ceiling* or a *cap*. Ceilings and caps are usually available on personal and residential loans. You may be able to get your lender to cap your commercial loan, i.e., the rate of interest shall be determined by ____, but will never be lower than ____ or higher than ____ .

Unless your crystal ball can predict the way interest rates are headed, there is no right answer to whether fixed or variable rates are better.

The usual rule is that borrowers pay more for fixed rate loans because lenders have bound themselves to a fixed rate and must protect themselves by charging more. Ultimately, the consumer pays for lender's margin of error and may in the long run pay more than if rates were adjustable.

Secured vs. non-secured loans

As discussed above, a secured loan offers lender collateral. On real estate, collateral is usually the house for which money has been borrowed. In theory, lenders charge less when loans are secured. The rationale behind this is that if the loan goes bad, the lender has additional recourse against the property. In actuality, this often is not the case. Lenders may in fact charge more for secured loans on investment property than for non-secured personal loans, i.e., personal lines of credit.

Investor vs. homeowner rate

When borrowing money to buy a house, two interest categories exist. The first type of interest is lower, long-term interest usually available for homeowners. The second type of interest is higher when banks label you an investor!

Your income as an investor may be the same as a homeowner. Your credit rating may be the same as a homeowner. The "investment" house may be identical to that of the "homeowner," and you may be putting the same percentage down. You might think the rates for your second house would be lower, especially since with your personal residence you have a greater combined equity.

Banks don't view it that way. Banks label you an investor, and while they may loan homeowners 80 percent of the appraised value, for investment homes, loans may be for only 70 percent of appraised value.

Banks believe people will do anything to save their personal residences, but are less vigilant managing "investment" property. Try to find a bank that considers investment property as a "second home" and charges the lower "homeowner" interest rate.

It is tempting not to tell the bank the property you are buying is investment property. However, one of the bank documents you will be signing is a statement that the loan is being made for home ownership, and specifically that you will occupy the house as your primary residence. Fraudulently signing this statement may be grounds for the bank to call the loan and require immediate full payment.

Preferred customer vs. regular customer

Some banks shave a point or two off interest for depositors maintaining minimum account balances, i.e. $2,500. Some banks will even let your IRA account qualify you as a preferred customer, though technically, IRA accounts cannot be used as loan collateral.

If friends or relatives have accounts at the bank, mention it. It is a negotiating item that you should not ignore. Large banks, however, could care less. Their investment money comes from other sources.

What you can negotiate on a mortgage

Lenders love bright, eager, new investors. New investors assume they lack power to negotiate the mortgage loan's many facets, including:

— points
— president's fee
— rate of interest
— teaser rates
— interest caps

— application fee
— balloon terms
— escrow terms
— choice of title company
— choice of surveyors, appraisers, etc.
— prepayment clauses
— adjustability of interest rate
— percentage down
— assumability.

I know someone who was "taken to the cleaners" by his bank on every single item listed above. He was not bitter. He called his first property his "learning house." But he was never taken to the cleaners again!

If possible, avoid using mortgages to finance your investment property. This chapter outlines other ways to obtain financing.

Why I am against mortgages

Application fee

Lenders charge significant application fees. If you recently purchased a house, the bank may have already performed an extensive credit check. The bank will waive a major portion of the credit application fee if you can convince them that only a credit *update* is needed.

Points

Landlords buying property via mortgages pay for many extra items. A most notorious item is *points*, also called loan discount, origination, or commitment fees.

A point equals 1 percent of the loan. For example, on a $50,000 loan with 3.5 points the bank charges $1,750 for the privilege of issuing the loan. Points are negotiable, especially since they are not out-of-pocket costs to the bank.

> *Note:* Sometimes, points work in your favor. It may be advantageous to offer to pay more points to secure a lower interest rate or other concessions from the bank.

President's fee

Another fee I know at least one bank charges is a 1 percent "President's Fee." This is in addition to a high loan origination fee. The president's fee goes straight to the bank president! Is this legal? Yes, this is for a commercial loan, although fees like this are the exception not the rule. What can you do about it? Say no!

Appraisal, surveying, and inspection

Banks require property appraisals to protect their investment, not yours. Besides paying for an appraisal, you also will pay for a property inspection, again for the lender, and for another person to survey the property.

—If there is an existing survey of recent origin, i.e., seller surveyed the property when he bought the property or when he put on a recent addition, you might be able to get the bank to accept seller's survey.

What's the difference between an appraiser and an inspector?

The inspector examines the different mechanical components to see that they work, i.e., air-conditioning, roof, foundation, etc. The appraiser values the property, i.e., the value of the land, the value of a two-story investment house in neighborhood X.

Note: Bank inspectors differ from the one you use when deciding to buy the property. Your inspector probes for defects affecting the value of house; the bank inspector just ascertains that the bank's interests are protected. While you have recourse against the inspector you chose for errors and omissions, you have little recourse, if any, against the bank's inspector.

Note the "weasel terms" inspectors employ. "No evidence of termite infestation seen," does not guarantee termite-free property, just that no termites were *seen*.

Bank's lawyers

Banks in effect require you to use their recommended attorneys. Bank's lawyers are usually more expensive than the attorney or title company you select. Banks pretend to offer you the choice of selecting your own attorney. But then they "sock it to you" by telling you that their attorney (at your expense) has to "review" whatever your attorney or title company prepared. Your attorney's quote that was $100 to 200 cheaper than the bank's lawyer is eroded when you have to pay the bank's attorney to "review" your attorney's work.

Time game

Another game banks play is the time game. Either by making it prohibitively expensive for you to use your own attorney or by the time game, lenders manage to get first-time borrowers to use higher priced bank attorneys. "Sure," they tell you, "you can use your own lawyer or title company, but, if you want the property closed by a certain date, we're not sure our attorney can finish 'review' by the time you need it." "But," they add, "if you use the bank's attorney, the necessary papers and title work will be ready by the time needed." (This happened on my first bank mortgage where I needed a year-end settlement. I swore I would never fall into this time trap again.)

While you have little control over bank attorneys' "review fees," you do have control over time. Where possible, avoid year-end closings, or allow ample time for banks and their attorneys to play the time game with you.

Prepayment Penalties

Prepayment is repaying the bank all the money owed before the end of the term. For example, prepayment on a twenty-five or thirty year mortgage occurs when you sell your property after the third year of ownership. Before you can pass title, mortgages have to be paid off.

State banking laws usually prohibit prepayment penalties on personal and home loans. That is why most consumers have never been hit with these penalties. However, since banks characterize your investment loan as "commercial," state laws prohibiting prepayment penalties do not apply. Banks can assess prepayment penalties as they wish.

> *Note*: Prepayment penalties are buried in the paragraph mounds of legalese fine print. Don't expect to see it neatly labeled, "PREPAYMENT PENALTY." Unless you specifically ask, the bank certainly will not bring it up.

The wording of my first property mortgage started innocently enough and then turned into a prepayment penalty. See if you can spot the prepayment penalty:

"This loan may be prepaid in whole or in part at any time, provided that the Mortgagee may collect twelve (12) months' advance interest on the aggregate amount of all prepayments made in any twelve-month period that exceed twenty percent (20%) of the amount of the original Mortgage;"

Prepayment penalties are added even if the *bank* demands prepayment. Wording from my first property mortgage:

"...said advance interest may be collected even though prepayment results from the Mortgagee (i.e., the bank-author) accelerating the loan and demanding payment in full as a result of a breach of any of the terms, covenants, or conditions of this mortgage."

> *Note*: To protect themselves, banks also insert another paragraph which doesn't make much sense at the loan's offset but becomes important later when they label the loan commercial. They insert phrases such as:
>
> "The loan is being made for the purpose of acquiring or carrying on a business or commercial investment within the meaning of _____ (the relevant section of your state code)."

Banks will hold you to prepayment provisions even if your initial loan rate was lower than what they can charge now. For example, the original rate was 8 percent, and now the rate is 12 percent. You would imagine that banks would encourage loan prepayment so they can use your repaid money to make higher rated loans. But banks do not work that way.

Even though the banks collected large loan origination fees and can now use your repaid money to make new (higher rate) loans and collect new loan origination fees, they still charge "prepayment" penalties which can amount to six to twelve months of interest. Since payments at the beginning of a loan term are mostly interest, that can be quite a bite.

For example, if a house is sold on year three of a thirty- year mortgage, and the prepayment penalty is six months' interest, the prepayment penalty on a $50,000 loan balance at 10.5 percent can amount to $2,577.01! If the bank penalizes you for twelve months interest, the penalty on a $50,000 loan balance can be over $5,000!

If your game-plan is to hold property a few years, there are a number of alternatives to avoiding or lowering the penalty:

—Negotiate when applying for the loan to have this provision waived. Since this is not an out-of-pocket expense to the bank, banks are sometimes agreeable. Use your best negotiating skills; remember this can be a $2,500 item, or more.

— Negotiate a smaller prepayment penalty, i.e., one or two months' interest. The key wording in all these prepayment clauses is, "The bank *may* charge." Banks have flexibility to be hard or easy.

— If you can swing it, pay off more principal each month, certainly from the time you envision selling. Banks allow you to pay small amounts of additional monthly principal without penalty. The more principal paid, the less interest.

— Ask the bank to waive the prepayment penalty in consideration for your using the proceeds for a new loan that you will be taking out. If you don't ask, you'll never get it.

I found out the hard way about prepayment penalties when I announced to the bank that I located a buyer for my recently purchased property and that I would be paying off my loan. My nice capital gain was diminished by a hefty prepayment penalty.

You can be sure that the second time I secured a bank mortgage, the prepayment clause was stricken from the onset. And that was the surprising part. After negotiating the terms of my second loan, I told the bank officer non-apologetically that the prepayment penalty clause must go. "No problem," he said, and he crossed it out!

The lesson to be learned from this prepayment story and every other negotiating point is to *speak up early*. Once your loan has been approved, it is too late.

Escrow accounts

If banks had their way, they would require funds to be escrowed for taxes, insurance, water levies, and a month or two's mortgage just in case you ever fall behind. I would say, sarcastically, if banks *really* had their way, they would require escrowing the *whole* loan.

While some jurisdictions require banks to pay interest on escrowed funds, the interest paid is usually below market and quite often is required only for residential loans, not commercial loans.

You can negotiate escrow terms. Perhaps you can get the bank to limit the escrow to taxes while you pay insurance. Perhaps you can get them to pay interest on the escrowed funds or increase the interest they pay.

The best arrangement I have seen is a bank that in effect credits escrowed money at the same interest rate as the loan, i.e., if the loan is for $50,000 and $1,000 is paid in escrow, the bank treats the $1,000 escrow as prepaid principal and charges interest only on $49,000. When the escrow is used, i.e., to pay taxes, the loan rises to the original $50,000.

You may not obtain your desired results, but the escrow account is one of your negotiation tools. Most people just assume escrow accounts are non-negotiable.

Balloon terms

Balloon terms are another way to secure low-rate financing. You can understand why banks hesitate to guarantee an interest rate for thirty years. On the other hand, you may have no intention of owning the property for thirty years. Your intention may be to sell the property after a few years. Together, you and the bank insert a balloon term. This keeps monthly payments down since payments are amortized over a thirty-year schedule, while at the same time assuring the bank that the loan will be repaid in an agreed amount of years.

> *Example*: John needs $100,000 to purchase and fix a house for sale within four years. John secures a 9 percent loan amortized over thirty years (to keep monthly payments low) with a four-year balloon. John's loan balloons, i.e., becomes due after the fourth year. John probably got a better deal than by going for a thirty-year, higher-rate mortgage, i.e., 10 percent.

Two-step loan

While balloon terms are still popular with private lenders, banks today are getting away from balloon terms. Banks realize that borrowers often are not able to sell their properties when balloon payments are due. Banks today use two-step loans called 5/25 or 7/23. Payments are amortized over thirty years, however, a low rate of interest is assured for the first five or seven years, and interest is renegotiated at the end of year five or seven. The renegotiated interest is usually set by an index, i.e., the rate paid on treasury bills, etc.

Example 1: Bank offers Sue a thirty-year mortgage at 9 percent.

Example 2: Bank offers Sue a 7/23 mortgage at 8.5 percent. Interest for the first seven years is set at 8.5 percent, and interest after year seven is renegotiated or determined by an arranged standard.

If Sue plans to sell the house before year seven, the terms in Example 2 might be better for her.

Teaser rates
These are low initial rates banks use to lure you to borrow from their bank.

Example: "Financing available at 7%!*"

Lure rates are in big capital numerals, while the subsequent rates are buried in the asterisk fine print.

Example: "These rates are in effect until April 28th, after which the interest rate is prime plus four points."

Sometimes, you can get the bank to extend the "sale" period, i.e., let you have the low rate for another six months to a year. Sometimes you cannot.

Lock-in rates
Some banks play games with lock-in rates. They agree to "lock-in" a low rate for say, sixty days, but then while rates are rising, they take more than sixty days to review the loan application. Once the sixty-day period expires, the bank demands a higher interest rate or additional points.

Because of effort and expense, most people do not litigate, even though they feel the bank acted without good faith. An effective means of getting justice (at least from borrower's standpoint) is to contact the State Banking Commission. Rather than open themselves to investigation, many banks will honor expired lock-in commitments.

Assumable loans

There is no reason why banks should not allow loans to be assumed by another qualified buyer in the event you have to sell. As you can see from real estate listings, an assumable loan is a selling point. Stress to the bank that this clause is important to you, and that you want an assumable loan without an escalation clause. You might even be able to use this as a trade off, i.e., you'll agree to a prepayment penalty clause as long as the loan is assumable. In this situation, you would not have to prepay the loan because the loan would be assumed by the new buyer. As with everything else, the bank may say no. But if you do not ask for the specific items in this chapter, you certainly will never get them.

Reducing your interest payments

Principal and interest are your biggest expenses. The portion of your monthly payment earmarked "principal" is really savings. The fun part of landlording is watching your invested principal (equity) increase each month.

Be realistic. Few rental properties generate sufficient income to finance both principal and interest. Most landlords are fortunate if rentals cover interest only. During the first few years, principal may have to be paid out of your own pocket. Call it forced savings. Only as rents increase and principal and interest remain constant will you be able to pay principal out of increased rents.

Rental property interest is still deductible, and that will probably never change. It helps at tax time because it is an expense that offsets income. But there are better ways to offset income. Property improvements, for example, also offset income, and at the same time add value to your property. It makes better sense to use rents for improvements than for interest payments.

If your interest rate is good, leave it alone. This is especially true if your interest rate is below the amount you can get on a Certificate of Deposit or other investment.

Most probably, your interest rate is high, especially if this is your first house. There is no need to apologize. All of us at one time fell in to the lender's trap.

Refinancing

Do not think that, if you already own investment property and have already secured the initial financing, nothing further can be done to lower payments.

The best way to lower investment property interest is to refinance your personal residence and take a larger first mortgage based on your increased equity. Unlike home equity loans which are really second mortgages, refinancing is still a first mortgage, and because the bank's stake is more secure with a first mortgage, it can charge a lower interest rate.

If you are going to mortgage your property, consider doing so *after* buying the property. (You are obviously going to have to get the initial purchase money from a different source. You may have to beg, borrow, or steal, but it can be done.) The advantage is that you are not rushed by time, and even with certain duplicating settlement expenses, you are in a better position to negotiate more favorable terms.

Guarantors

Investors and corporations sometimes use guarantors to secure cheaper interest terms. Guarantors are multi-million dollar companies guaranteeing loans as a business.

Example: A bank lends $100,000 to an investor at prime plus five points. (The bank obviously considers the investor or loan risky.) If the investor gets a guarantor acceptable to the bank to guarantee the loan, the bank's risk is lessened, and the bank can lend money at a substantially cheaper rate, i.e., prime plus two points.

Individuals can try a variation of this.

Example: Sally needs a $50,000 loan. Because she is a risk, the bank demands high interest. Sally's dad agrees to serve as guarantor. (*Why* friends and relatives agree to serve as guarantors is a separate matter.) Since the bank's risk is lessened, Sally should enjoy a lower interest rate.

Offering a larger down payment to reduce interest

Because leverage is king in real estate, experts advise putting the least down as down payment. They reason with certain logic that it is best to conserve assets for future projects.

That said, you can sometimes negotiate a lower interest rate where you increase your personal stake in the property through a larger down payment. Start your negotiation offering the least amount down. Then ante the down payment upward. Never voluntarily offer a large percentage down. Like everything else in this chapter, if you do not ask for a reduced interest rate because you will be putting down a larger down payment, the bank will not volunteer this.

Home equity loans

If residential mortgages provide the cheapest form of financing, home equity loans provide the second cheapest form of financing. Home equity loans are lines of credit secured by your home's unmortgaged equity.

> *Example*: Mary's residence, valued at $120,000, has an existing $60,000 mortgage. Mary can obtain a home equity line of credit, usually for about 75 percent of the unmortgaged equity, in this case $45,000.

Some people call these loans second mortgages; others avoid the term, since with home equity loans you do not have to use the funds available in your line of credit.

By whatever name you call it, you still pay for a new title search, lien sheets, appraisal, inspection, documentary stamps, and recording fees. In theory, loan approval time is quicker.

Unlike conventional loans, home equity loans afford very little negotiating room. It is a package banks offer; the best you can do is to compare loans and take a loan with the most favorable features.

What to look for in a home equity line of credit

—*Low interest*. While the usual rate is prime plus two points, some banks offer prime plus one point, and even prime plus three-quarters points. Some banks offer attractive fixed rates for a set amount of years, and some banks allow you to "lock-in" to a fixed rate.

Note: Again, beware of introductory teaser rates, i.e., 8 percent for the first six months, and then buried in a footnote is the substantially higher rate the loan assumes.

—*Interest caps.* Some banks offer interest rate caps, i.e., loan interest cannot exceed a certain maximum. The downside is that interest caps are usually accompanied by interest floors, i.e., even if the prime goes way down, rates can never be lower than a certain base amount.

—*Open-ended, interest only,* i.e., no set repayment schedule. You may pay off principal, but are not required to do so. Caution: Be wary of balloon payment terms, or you may find yourself in a situation where you have to sell assets to satisfy balloon terms.

—*Bank pays all or most of closing costs.* Banks are in keen competition. Some banks rebate all or most of closing costs. Some banks condition the rebate to your actually using the line of credit, i.e., banks want you not only to have a line of credit, but to *use* it.

—*Home equity loans that accept other collateral besides your personal residence.* You may have to look, but you will find banks making home equity loans on second homes and investment properties.

Advantages of using home equity lines of credit
—*Ready cash.* You pay only for money you use. When the right deal arises, you have money to invest. No questions are asked.

—*Pay off higher priced loans,* i.e., unsecured lines of credit. Interest on home equity loans is significantly cheaper than on other forms of loans, and interest, unlike on personal loans, can be tax-deductible.

—*Speed.* Processing home equity loans usually takes less time than conventional secured loans.

Disadvantages to using home equity lines of credit
—*Liability.* If the investment goes sour, you risk losing your primary residence on which the loan was secured.

—*Variable interest rates can skyrocket.* Remember a number of years back when the prime approached 21 percent? A prime- plus-two-points loan would drive most landlords to the poor house.

—*IRS cap.* At this writing, the IRS allows home equity debt of $100,000 ($50,000 for a married person filing separately), and the loan cannot exceed the house's fair market value. This may limit the amount of borrowed money.

—*Questionable bank requirements.* For a home equity line, a friend of mine still had to pay for a termite inspection, despite the fact that his home was on the sixteenth floor of a cement, high-rise condominium. Other banks require property surveys to be redone, despite the fact that a house inspection shows that neither you nor your neighbors have done anything to change the existing property boundaries.

—*Refinancing.* If you have considerable equity in the house, it may be cheaper to refinance your original mortgage. A home equity loan is still a second mortgage, and second mortgage rates are usually higher than first mortgage rates. Too, home equity interest rates are almost always variable, while refinanced first mortgage loans can be fixed.

Alternate forms of financing

To the extent refinancing can lead to lower monthly mortgage payments, this is an area that landlords cannot ignore.

Lines of credit

Admittedly, lines of credit are harder to secure now than years ago. But they are available in amounts between generally $15,000 and $50,000. Interest rates are usually quite reasonable, i.e., a point or two above prime. There are no prepayment penalties or required escrow accounts. The drawbacks are that lines of credit have variable interest rates, lines are reviewed annually, and some banks charge annual maintenance fees ($15 to $25). While it is unusual, lines of credit can be lowered or canceled for no reason. Try to obtain as many different lines of credit as you can. Just because you have a credit line does not mean you have to use it, assuming you're not the type of person who will blow it all in Las Vegas.

Some people obtain lines of credit in two stages. For stage one, they obtain application forms from every available bank. They do not limit themselves to their own city. They get applications from all in-state banks and even out of state. After all, banks are now regional, and they all use computerized credit services.

For stage two, they mail all applications on the same day. The reason for this is that banks contact credit bureaus who insert the name of the inquiring bank at the bottom of the credit report. A bank will want to know why you sent out twenty different applications. By mailing all applications the same day, you can often beat the credit bureau entries.

Is this fraud? Attorneys I have asked say no. Banks can find out soon enough about multiple applications, and they can always revoke credit lines.

If a bank turns you down, keep trying. Find out who at the bank turned you down. Work with them or go over their heads. Try every bank in the phone book. Different banks use different credit bureau services, and not all credit reports contain the same information. I have learned one thing over the years that defies logic. For every bank that turns you down, another bank will accept you!

Credit reports

If your application is denied, you are entitled to a free copy of the credit report the bank used to make its determination. Every person in the United States should examine his credit report. It is chock-full of the most useless and outdated information, not to mention absolutely incorrect information. It has you working at jobs you no longer work and at salaries you no longer make. It lists current loans long since paid and excludes current loans. It also lists "nuisance liens."

Example: A friend's application for a multi-hundred-thousand- dollar loan was held up over a $10 shirt! Years earlier, my friend refused to pay a department store bill because the shirt he bought was damaged. He claimed he returned the shirt, the store said he didn't, and they informed the credit bureau of his non-payment.

The bank refused to process the loan while this item was pending. The $10 dispute eventually was straightened out, but only after numerous phone calls and letters while a multi-hundred-thousand-dollar deal was in limbo.

Mortgages to yourself as a form of protection

A mortgage can actually protect you. On this one, you may have to speak with an accountant or lawyer to make sure it is done right.

Example: Tom uses his personal line of credit to buy a $50,000 rental property which will be owned by Tom's corporation, Acme Properties, Inc. Ordinarily, no mortgage is created since Tom buys the property for cash. Acme pays Tom monthly, but the debt to Tom is unsecured. Catastrophe strikes when tenant Sam Suer is awarded $50,000. For the sake of this example, Acme's insurance carrier refuses to pay the claim.

Acme may lose its sole $50,000 asset (the property) to satisfy the $50,000 judgment. Tom still has to pay for his loan, because Tom's interest was unsecured. When Tom lent Acme the $50,000 to purchase the property, Tom should have obtained a $50,000 mortgage from Acme, which, properly recorded, can take precedence over the subsequent judgment.

Mortgage brokers

Mortgage brokers, like real estate agents, are intermediaries. Whereas real estate agents bring buyers and sellers together, mortgage brokers bring borrowers and lenders together. Through their contacts, they help buyers secure loans at the best rates and terms. One catchy slogan reads: "From application to closing, we're by your side." As many as 37 percent of all federally insured mortgages originate with mortgage brokers.

Some states regulate/license mortgage brokers; some do not. Some brokers belong to the National Association of Mortgage Brokers; others do not.

Ideally, fees are paid by lenders. In reality, brokers charge borrowers application processing fees, fees for credit checks, appraisals, and points, i.e., 1- 1.5 points when securing the loan. This also is known as a commitment fee.

Some people claim they could not have secured loans without a mortgage broker. Conversely, some people claim that in hindsight, they could have secured loans themselves. Pros and cons for using mortgage brokers are similar to pros and cons for using real estate agents.

Advantages

—Mortgage brokers broker for a living and are up-to-date on lenders, lending practices, and lending sources.

—Through their contacts and volume, brokers can obtain better rates and terms than buyers can secure themselves.

—Brokers help borrowers prepare applications and wade through

the maze of questions.
—Brokers answer borrower and lender questions. They negotiate to get the deal settled.

Disadvantages
—With work, some borrowers can secure equally advantageous loans without incurring broker fees.
—Brokers overwhelmed with work may delay work on particular loans, whereas borrowers advancing their own cause press lenders until the loan is approved.
—Brokers may not in fact steer you to lending institutions with the best rates or terms, i.e., brokers may steer you to institutions giving *them* the best commissions.
—Brokers may take up-front, non-refundable processing fees from people who have no realistic chance of getting a loan.

Owner financing
If you were not able to secure owner financing *before* you purchased the property, consider doing so *after* you purchase the property. It can be from the seller or anyone else with money to lend.

Example: Seller wants cash for his property and buyer takes out a mortgage. Seller put the cash in the bank and receives, say, 5 percent interest. Buyer is paying 12 percent on his commercial mortgage. Buyer approaches the seller and offers 9 percent. Buyer pays off his higher loan and gives the lender a first mortgage in the loaned amount. Seller now earns higher interest than at the bank while buyer's interest rate drops from 12 percent to 9 percent.

CHAPTER 9

INSURANCE

Should you insure?

Lenders require property insurance for at least the mortgage amount, so there is little leeway there. If you borrow $50,000, lenders require at least $50,000 of property insurance listing lender as prime beneficiary in case of disaster.

As for liability insurance, majority opinion is to secure insurance in the largest amount you can afford or the largest amount you feel at risk. The reasons for this are obvious, and liability insurance is not overly expensive.

A minority opinion recommends against securing liability insurance. Minority opinion reasons that, if plaintiffs' lawyers know landlords have no liability insurance, lawyers would think twice before commencing suit, as there is less of a "deep pocket." Landlords would be less apt to settle to avoid suit, as insurance companies are prone to do. Recovering judgments would be more difficult.

Before following this course, realize that liability insurance serves another function—it also pays for landlord's legal defense. This is no small item, especially as defense lawyers charge high hourly fees and over eighteen million lawsuits (a.k.a. "suit-cases") are filed in state courts each year. Until the legal climate in this country changes, consider liability insurance a necessary business cost.

Should you keep insurance policies separate?

There are advantages and disadvantages to keeping all insurance coverage (home, health, auto, investment property) on one master policy or with one agent.

Advantages to using one company or agent
—You deal with one agent who has a good grasp of your entire financial structure, not several agents who know only certain facets of your activities.
—You may get a combined better deal from one agent or carrier than if your policies were with separate carriers, i.e., some carriers offer multiple-policy discounts.
—Having several policies with one company may guarantee better service. A company that might drop you for filing a claim might think twice if other policies are involved.

Advantages to using different companies and agents
—*Spread the risk.* You can switch to other companies, if one company goes out of business, cancels policies in certain territories, drastically raises rates, or changes coverage.
—*Better cash flow.* Some companies require the year's insurance premiums in advance, while others bill quarterly or semi-annually. Using different companies allows you to spread payments over the year for better cash flow.
—*Lower premiums.* You can pick and choose carriers with the lowest premiums for each category. Use one company for the best auto rates, another for the best homeowner rates, etc. The chances of one company offering the best rates for every category are slim.

Independent agents vs. company agents
Independent agents, also known as general agents or brokers, do not act on behalf of any one company. They are authorized to sell insurance for many different companies. Independent agents have a good grasp of who is writing what and comparative premiums. Coverage is not effective until the insurance company has agreed to accept the risk. Insurance binders however, serve as temporary insurance until the policy is written or disapproved.

Company agents represent one company, i.e., Allstate agents represent Allstate. They do not sell insurance for other companies.

A good thing about company agents is that they transact business on behalf of the insurance company. This means that you are covered as soon as the agent accepts your premiums. Nevertheless, since insurance policies are written by insurance companies, there is always self-protecting language allowing companies to terminate a previously written policy, i.e., the insurance company home office always reserves the right to terminate policies, even those written by its agents.

Independent agents represent *you*, while company agents represent the company. Understand that when talking to the "friendly" company agent.

What's best for you?

Many investors prefer independent agents because they do not push the policy of any single company and can recommend the best coverage for your needs.

In reality, independent agents still have their preferred companies and steer you to their favorite companies.

There are hundreds of insurance companies out there all vying to insure homeowners. With investment property, the field narrows. Companies insuring your home are not anxious to insure investment property, especially property at the low end, and when they do, there may be many conditions and exclusions. Sometimes commercial coverage is better suited for your property.

Make inquiries of both general agents and company agents, and don't overlook commercial coverage. Your job is to secure the most coverage *that you require*, at the best price.

> *Note*: "(t)hat you require" is italicized. Just because you over insure property does not mean that you collect the insured high amount. You may be paying extra premiums for no reason.

Name insurance companies

This is an age where advertised brands triumph over non-advertised brands. Some insurance companies widely advertise and are household names. Some companies do not advertise and are relatively unknown to the public.

Every now and then, consumer groups such as *Consumer Reports* rate different companies. Rated categories include premiums, payouts, time spent processing claims, overall customer satisfaction, etc. Some of the best performers are "no-name" companies, while some "popular" companies fall at the bottom of the list. You do not have to stick with the "brand names."

How insurance companies rate property

Companies assign different ratings to different categories based on their loss experience. Sometimes, quotes differ between companies solely because of ratings companies assign to insured property.

> *Example:* On a three-unit building, one insurance company may rate a building as an apartment house, while to another insurance company, an apartment house is four or more units.

It makes a difference whether your property is rated "investment property," "second home," or "four properties or less."

The investment property label

The least desirable insurance category (highest premiums) is investment property, especially "low-end" investment property, as your first house is apt to be. Insurance companies loathe landlords with many investment properties, particularly if property is located in "rough" areas. Insurance companies prefer concentrating on homeowners' coverage. Low-end investment property is handled only as an accommodation.

Some companies feel that landlords with more than four properties are "in business." Some companies believe landlords with many investment properties, especially in "rough" areas, make fewer repairs and concentrate on quantity (number of houses) and not quality.

Some insurance companies have special rates for landlords with four properties or less, again, as a special accommodation. They reason that with less than four properties a person is still an average homeowner and is not involved in a "landlording" business.

Bidding wars

People understand bidding wars on automobile purchases. After you get a dealer's best quote, you ask another dealer to beat it. Experts recommend doing the same with insurance companies. To some extent it works and you can get a better quote.

But there is a difference between auto dealers and insurance agents. You generally deal only once with an auto dealer; after signing the papers, you have no further dealings. With insurance companies, you do have further dealings. Besides price, you want your insurance agent to be accessible, understandable, and accurate. Besides price, you want a company that efficiently handles claims and processes payments.

As your investment portfolio increases, you want a company to go to bat for you. Perhaps a policy accidentally lapsed, or a claim is somewhat questionable. Some companies let preferred customers pay premiums over the course of the year without imposing interest penalties. As you can see, it is sometimes better to overpay in order to get preferred customer service.

Taking over a prior owner's policy

Some advice books advise against taking over a prior owner's policy. The reason is because prior owners generally have their property underinsured or not covered for items new owners prefer. This advice makes certain sense on homeowners policies. It makes less sense on investment property.

—*Availability*. In many areas of the country, you cannot get insurance to cover certain items, i.e., hazardous materials. If the former owner's policy covers the items you want, there is no reason to let it lapse.

—*Documentation*. Insurance companies want photographs for investment properties and need all sorts of information. If they already insure the property, photographs and supplemental information may not be required.

—*Continuity*. If you were to have a claim during the first year, a company that has insured the property over the years can view the claim on a larger basis before deciding whether to renew your policy or raise your rates.

Note: As discussed below, when taking over a prior owner's policy, the policy must be is rewritten to cover the new owner's interest.

Photographs

Insurance companies often require that photographs of the property (usually front and back) accompany the insurance application.

Don't succumb to the agent's offer to photograph the property. Do it yourself. While photographs should not be deceptive, you are permitted to photograph a house from the best angle. Pick a sunny day to shoot. If the house is vacant, you do not have to aim your camera to show bare windows or a "for rent" sign. If the yard is a mess, aim up a bit. If the insurance company is not satisfied with your photographs, they can always have their agent take pictures.

> *Note*: For larger properties, experts recommend having the insurance company inspect the property *before* signing the sales contract, or alternatively that the sales contract be contingent upon the insurance company agreeing to insure. This makes sense when stakes are high. Why wait till you actually own the property to find that securing insurance may be problematic?

Advance insurance company inspection also gives buyer extra leverage, i.e., buyer can require seller to fix property to conform to insurance requirements.

Which names must go on the policy?
While your accountant or lawyer may recommend that property be titled in a corporate or partnership name, some insurance companies insure only property titled in an individual name. The reason for their "pickiness" is insurance companies are not looking to insure businesses which often have additional liability exposure.

> *Note*: Some companies allow a variation of private and multi-party ownership, i.e. "John Jones, t/a (trading as) Jones Realty, Inc."

Make sure title and policy names agree.
Insurance companies may deny coverage if the policy name differs from the name on the title. This can affect representation and recovery.
In the above example, if house title is in the name of Jones Realty, Inc., the insurance policy also must be in that name. Investors sometimes forget this when they insure investment property under their master homeowner's policy which is in an individual, not a corporate, name.

Always add names.
For extra caution, if property is titled in a corporate name, make sure your name and the person managing your property is also on the policy. If an accident occurs, plaintiff's lawyers will probably sue you

as manager, or the person managing the property for you as well as the owner of the house. Therefore, if the house is owned by Jones Realty, Inc., and you and your brother manage the property, make sure the liability policy covers Jones Realty, Inc., you, and your brother.

There is usually no added charge for extra names on a policy, but failure to have all possible names on a policy can make the difference between a company representing you or not.

Transfer of title

Some people become landlords by happenstance, for example, they inherit rental property or acquire property in a divorce settlement. Because the former owner's insurance policy is still in effect, new owners often fail to inform the insurance company of the ownership change. Sometimes, new owners continue paying the former owner's premiums without ever changing the policy name.

Big mistake. When a fire or accident occurs, insurance companies will shy from coverage under the "sale or alienation clause" buried in the pages of gobbledygook. Insurance companies do not like it when there is a change of title interest by "sale or alienation," and they seize the chance to deny coverage.

Conditional sale of property

Questions arise when a landlord sells a house to a tenant but holds legal title until the tenant finishes making payments. There have been cases affirming the insurance company's denial of coverage because there has been a "sale or alienation," even though landlord still has legal title. Unfortunately, these situations are often *Catch-22* since tenant cannot secure a homeowner's policy in his own name because house title is still in landlord's name; i.e., tenant does not have "sole and unconditional ownership" which insurance companies require to insure property.

Sale of property

Similar problems arise when a fire or accident occurs after owner signs a contract of sale. Insurance companies try to escape from coverage since the owner no longer has "sole and unconditional ownership." Their position is made stronger when owner accepts part of the purchase price as a deposit giving buyer an "insurable interest."

Law books have pages of annotations covering these situations and, as you can imagine, cases go many ways. Unfortunately, you must be constantly on guard when dealing with insurance companies. When title to property changes in any way, you must resolve this change with the insurance company.

Deductibles

On fire coverage, it is usually cheaper to carry a larger policy with a larger deductible, i.e., a $1,000 deductible instead of the usual $250 or $500 deductibile. You benefit most if the house totally burns but benefit least if there is a small fire.

Limited fire damage, i.e., less than $1,000, may not substantially impair your investment property. A fire this size will mostly affect your tenant's personal possessions which are not covered under your policy in any event. More importantly, collecting insurance money on small fires also may jeopardize your insurability. Landlords for this reason often absorb small losses while benefiting from the savings realized by large deductibles.

Vacant vs. unoccupied

Some insurance policies exclude "vacant" houses from fire coverage. What is a vacant house? What vacancy *should* mean is a house is not rentable. Such houses are most prone to vandalism and fire damage. Companies differ on this point.

At what point is a house vacant? There is no single answer. An insurance company may argue that a house is vacant between tenants. Some insurance policies state that a house is vacant after thirty days. This can be a problem when it takes more than thirty days to clean and rent a house. There may not be much you can do about this; however, knowledge of this limitation may spur you to renovate or rent at a faster pace, or secure an insurance rider allowing for a longer vacancy period.

Vandalism

People assume that insurance covers vandalism. Too often, it is excluded within the paragraphs of legalese gobbledygook. While vandalism occurs less frequently in owner-occupied dwellings, vandalism is not uncommon in investment property, especially when unoccupied.

Note: Just because you paid for vandalism and malicious mischief protection, this does not mean that you can collect if your house is vandalized. Insurance companies still believe that no restitution is due when the vandalized house was vacant and/or unoccupied.

While you have little negotiating power with insurance carriers on this matter, know in advance if you have coverage. If lack of coverage bothers you, let your agent suggest appropriate coverage.

Theft

Excluded also from the basic landlords' fire/liability policy is theft. Besides vandalism, vacant houses are also theft targets. Theft items include hot water heaters, furnaces, sinks, refrigerators, copper piping, bathroom appliances, light fixtures, and ceiling fans. Landlord horror stories go further: doors, fireplace mantels, windows, paneling, thermostats, etc.

The key to all this is that you are not insured through your basic landlord's fire/liability policy. As with vandalism, if lack of coverage bothers you, ask your agent to suggest broader, "all-risk" coverage.

Consequential loss

Besides fire and liability insurance, you also want your policy to contain consequential loss provisions. One consequential loss you will have if your investment property becomes unrentable is no rental income, even though you still have to pay the mortgage and taxes. Consequential loss provisions in your policy assure rental payments while you renovate.

Note: Insurance companies require proof of tenant occupancy before the fire, as well as proof of their payments. A copy of the lease or rent book should suffice.

Consequential losses are limited to "fair" rental value and are usually offset by expenses the landlord does not incur while the property is vacant.

Example: If rent is $500 a month and landlord pays for heat, consequential loss will be $500 less the monthly heating cost.

Other consequential loss provisions are provisions for debris removal, demolition, and fire department service charges. Removal of fire debris and demolition, can amount to thousands of dollars over and above renovation costs. Similarly, as more municipalities charge users for government services, owners suffering fire loss, may find themselves indebted to local jurisdictions, for expenses incurred in putting out the fire. Sometimes these costs are not covered by your regular policy. If these items are important to you, you must secure appropriate coverage.

Replacement value

By now, most informed people know to ask for replacement coverage. The reason for this is that if a working, ten-year-old refrigerator is destroyed, it has to be replaced. Because new models are several hundred dollars, you want more than the $50 book value the insurance company offers for a ten-year-old refrigerator. You want replacement value on investment property also. Be wary of the term "market value." It is *not* the same as replacement value. The "market value" of a ten-year-old refrigerator is $50. That is not what you want.

Additions/alterations

Problems sometimes occur when landlords fix up property and subsequent loss ensues.

Example 1: John bought a vacant house with an unfinished basement. John subsequently enlarged the rear of the house, added a front and rear porch, and finished the basement.

Example 2: John bought a vacant house and subdivided it into three apartments.

Again, insurance companies notoriously try to weasel out of coverage. Whether they are justified depends on which side of the fence you sit. The prudent course to follow is to alert your insurance company of your action and allow them to determine whether they wish to continue coverage or increase premiums.

Videotaping

Videotaping the house and especially its contents is recommended for homeowners' policies. Policies covering investment property do not generally insure personal property, and the need for videotaping is not as great. Nevertheless, a careful investor will videotape the inside and outside of his investment property to settle any future contention.

> *Note*: Another videotaping benefit might be in rent court or small claims court to support a landlord's claim concerning the way a house looked before (and after) a particular tenant's tenancy.

Must you read the insurance policy?

Harsh as it sounds, the answer is yes. Law books are full of cases where policies covered the wrong address or omitted an address. Law books are full of cases where the insured thought coverage was for one amount, while the policy covered a different amount. When the inevitable happens, i.e., disaster strikes, insurance companies notoriously try to escape from representation and coverage.

While ultimately there may be some recourse against the agent who wrote the policy, the burden of proof is on you.

Take a few extra minutes when you get a policy to see that it covers the right address, specifies the right names, and lists the agreed coverage. Also, hold on to your policies, probably forever. When disaster strikes, everyone looks to you for a copy of your policy.

Other types of insurance

Mortgage insurance

Banks may suggest insurance that will continue to pay your mortgage if you are deceased, disabled, or unemployed. Most people are savvy enough to know that this insurance is generally overpriced and chock full of exclusions. You can secure better insurance privately.

Title insurance

You are advised to secure title insurance by every knowledgeable real estate authority and especially by real estate lawyers and title companies. Banks and lending institutions require lender's title insurance as well. In some states, title insurance costs are borne by sellers, in other states by buyers.

Title insurance protects buyers against title defects, i.e., if there was a forgery in the chain of title or the property was sold by a person lacking title. The public is told to buy title insurance because it is a one-time charge and not expensive in relation to the property price. Almost everyone, myself included, complies.

Yet, I have spoken with numerous lawyers and title companies. While lawyers and title companies can conjure up situations where title insurance could come to use, hardly anyone could recall a case where someone ever collected on a title policy. Based on what title companies pay out, title insurance should cost pennies. Instead, policies cost several hundred dollars, and lawyers and title companies continue to collect hefty commissions. Moreover, if you sell the property after a short time, the new owner has to buy an entirely new policy. In my opinion, this is truly an industry ripe for investigation.

Furnace contracts

A landlord's greatest fear is a tenant's midnight call that the furnace died. Murphy's Law assures that calls come during sub-freezing temperatures and twenty-two inches of snow, when no serviceman is available.

See if your utility company issues furnace contracts. It should be less than $75 a year, and some charge the same rates for tenant-occupied houses as homeowner houses.

Be sure to enroll during open season. At other times, there may be a special processing fee, or the company may require the furnace to be examined at your cost. Your peace of mind is worth the annual fee, and of course, if the furnace needs only one call a year, you are ahead of the game with your annual fee.

> *Note*: If you are not getting a service contract, consider acquiring an inexpensive electric space heater to loan tenants when the furnace is out of order. This can be a tremendous landlord aid.

Hot water heater contracts

Service contracts for hot water heaters also can be obtained. Know, however, that many hot water heater parts are not covered under these contracts. Using a cost-benefit analysis, your better bargain is with a furnace contract. However, if you seek peace of mind, consider also a water heater contract.

CHAPTER 10

TAXES:
KEEPING MORE OF WHAT YOU EARN

Part I
Income Taxes

Your strategy is *avoidance*, not evasion, as you try to *maximize* expenses and *minimize* income within the bounds of law. Since tax laws constantly change, use this chapter as a guide.

Lowering income
Acceptable ways to lower or postpone rental income
—If a tenant improves property, it is not income to you unless the improvement is in lieu of rent.

Example: Tenant builds a shelving unit into a closet or installs a backyard fence to improve the property.

—You are on a cash reporting calendar year, and your tenant defers paying December's rent to the following year. (Caution: Do this only with extremely trustworthy tenants.)

—An expanded variation of this is to have rent due at the end of the term (i.e., next year or sometime in the future). Remember, as discussed in chapter six, contrary to popular belief, rent is normally due at the *end* of the term.

Note: To protect yourself, arrange some sort of security deposit even if it is a non-liquid asset. This is attractive to cash-strapped tenants. They conserve cash by placing non-liquid assets as security; you may be in a position to defer income to another year.
  The IRS imposes certain limitations on deferred income that go beyond the scope of this book, i.e., deferred payments

exceeding $250,000.

—If you rent your vacation home less than fifteen days a year, rental income is not taxable, but rental deductions are not allowed.
—Capital gains on the sale of investment property may be deferred using the *installment* sales method.

Example: If Frank bought investment property for $100,000 and sells it five years later for $150,000, Frank pays capital gains on $50,000 in the year of the sale.

If, however, Frank sold the property via an *installment* method, i.e., over fifteen years, Frank's capital gain is spread over fifteen years.

> *Note*: There are installment sale caveats that go beyond the scope of this book. Limitations apply when the sales price exceeds a certain amount, i.e. $150,000, when seller is a dealer in property, and when accelerated depreciation has been taken.

Non-acceptable ways to lower income
— tenants paying landlord's property taxes, interest, insurance, or utilities. To the extent tenants make these payments, it is rental income to landlord.
— tenants performing services in lieu or partial lieu of rent, i.e., tenants responsible for snow removal or lawn work when such responsibility is landlord's. The IRS adds the fair market value of tenant service to the rent.
— landlord performing services that are normally tenant's responsibility, i.e., maid service. The IRS may force you to allocate between rent and maid service, and to boot, may require you as landlord to pay self-employment taxes on that part of the rental income which was for service not related to the property.

Maximizing Expenses
Acceptable ways to maximize expenses
—*Children*. Pay your children to perform legitimate functions for you. Depending on their tax bracket, children either pay no taxes or are taxed at a lower rate. Tax experts recommend paying

children with a business check and keeping records of work performed.

(Conceivably, work permits may be required when employing children. When paying children, make sure you don't run afoul of other reporting requirements, i.e., W-2s.)

—*Office equipment.* Don't go overboard. Just because you bought your first piece of investment real estate does not mean you have to impress the IRS with your new home office, maid service, fax machine, paper shredder, trash compactor, seminars, car phone, and subscriptions to a half dozen business journals. Eventually all these items will be deductible. Don't raise unnecessary eyebrows your first year.

—*Executive perks.* Don't be a pig. Just because you bought your first piece of income-producing property does not mean you can justify travel, conventions, country clubs, medical insurance, meals, and entertainment. No one item is verboten. But unless you have the income to go with these expenses, the IRS tolerates only so much loss before getting picky.

Note: The IRS is getting ever more picky:

Gifts and meals have new limitations, i.e., $25 per recipient for gifts and only a percentage of meals are tax-deductible. (They also have to be fully documented.)

Phones. No longer can you apportion your home telephone basic service between business and personal use and deduct the business portion.

Computers and office equipment. Must be used more than 50 percent for business. Straight-line depreciation must be used; no more accelerated depreciation.

—Lease equipment rather than buying it. Lease payments are deductible expenses. For example, if you use a vehicle exclusively for business, leasing may make more sense than buying it outright.

Non-acceptable ways of maximizing property expenses
—Itemizing in the year paid special assessments for paving, sewer systems, and local improvements. These are not taxes or repairs; the IRS calls these items capital improvements that must be added

to the property basis.

—Itemizing insurance in the year paid, if the covered period exceeds a year. Insurance must be prorated to cover the specific tax year.

—Beginning depreciation when the house is not ready for tenants, i.e., you buy the house in January and spend February and March fixing it up. Depreciation begins in April when the house is ready for renting.

—When repairs are part of a larger renovation/improvement project, the repair portion is a capital expense.

Example: John spends $50,000 during the year to rehab a building. The entire amount is a capital expense even though part of the expense went for regular repairs, i.e., replacing broken windows, cleaning, painting, etc. Tax experts recommend scheduling renovation over a period of years.

—Paying real estate taxes to the bank. While you may prepay real estate taxes, prepayment to a bank's escrow mortgage account is not prepaid real estate taxes. Taxes are deductible only when actually paid by the bank.

—Buyer paying seller's back taxes. Buyer's payment is added to the cost basis of the house.

Home office

While taking a home office deduction in general raises IRS eyebrows, it may be harder for you to do so for "property management."

Quite simply, to claim a home office deduction, you must prove that the home activity constitutes a business or a trade.

Is owning a single house a business or trade? What about five or fifteen houses? What if property income is your sole source of income?

The IRS has taken the position that property management is an "income-producing" activity akin to managing investments and has denied the home office deduction to people who raised the same arguments that you are probably considering.

You are probably thinking that you have another job and your home is the only place where you can conduct your personal property affairs. The courts will rule in your favor if your activities "rise to the level" of a business. There is no magic number as to how many properties you must manage before your activities are viewed as a business and not merely an investment.

There are two types of home office expenses. The first is avoidable or out-of-pocket expenses for equipment, i.e., furniture and office machinery. The second goes further and apportions the residence's overall avoidable expenses devoted to the office, i.e., a portion of the house's total taxes, insurance, cleaning, utilities, etc. Apportionment can either be based on square footage or on the number of rooms used for business.

Some people go further and depreciate the percentage of the house used for business purposes, i.e., if one-sixth of the house is used for business and the house is worth $180,000, they depreciate $30,000 (one-sixth of the house's value). Besides the extra bookkeeping and accounting costs, it complicates things years down the road when you sell the house and have to transfer the basis or determine capital gains.

It might be better not to take this deduction but rather use it as leverage against the IRS if audited. Sure, you might argue to the IRS, "I will file an amended return to reflect X, Y, or Z, but my amended return will also now take home office depreciation and the IRS will not realize a single additional cent." This sometimes works.

Repairs vs. renovations

The general rule is that repair expenses are tax-deductible in the year spent while renovation expenses are amortized over a period of years. Simplified even more, big items must be depreciated over a period of years while little items can be fully deducted immediately.

Casualty and theft loss

Unlike individual returns where casualty and theft items are subject to a deductible and must exceed a certain percentage of adjusted gross income, casualty and theft losses can be deducted from rental income.

Passive activities

Whether or not you think it's fair, under the 1986 tax revisions, real estate activity is deemed a *passive activity* subject to a $25,000 annual loss limitation.

Two criteria govern—*management* and *income*:
    —You must be actively involved in real estate management, *and*

—The $25,00 loss limitation is income related, i.e., for combined adjusted gross income over $150,000 you cannot take any losses, and between $100,000 and $150,000 you can deduct only $1 for every $2 of losses.

Note: Consider filing separate returns, i.e., Jane's income is $75,000 and Dick's is $60,000. If Dick actively participates in real estate, it may pay for the couple to file separately so that Dick can enjoy the $25,000 loss limitation which would be lessened if the couple filed jointly.

You are considered to actively manage property if you have a responsibility for such things as approving major repairs, selecting tenants, and establishing rents, even if you use a management company.

Another way to partially circumvent the $25,000 limitation is to buy property via a home equity loan or through refinancing your personal residence. Interest in most instances is totally deductible, i.e., you can deduct interest *and* the $25,000 allowable loss.

Example 1: Your properties have $30,000 in net losses. You can jointly deduct only $25,000 because of the $25,000 passive loss limitation.

Example 2: Your properties have $30,000 in net losses, but $5,000 of these losses are additional interest payments on your residence that you refinanced in order to purchase the investment property. You can jointly deduct the $25,000 passive loss *and* the $5,000 in interest.

Filing

I always file on or before April 15, but audit pros tell you to apply for an extension and wait until October 15 to file.

Why? Their reasoning is that by August the IRS has decided how many returns to audit. By October, auditors are piled high with April returns and only briefly review October filings. Your audit chances are said to be less.

IRS Labels

A popular myth is that you should not use the pre-printed coded label on tax forms because it tips off the IRS to _____ (fill in your worst fear). Tax guides, even those written by former IRS agents, dismiss this myth as bunk. The label's only use is to guide your return to the proper station to speed processing.

Tax return preparation

While the average person can no longer deduct expenses for tax return preparation, the IRS allows as a legitimate rental expense, expenses relating to preparing specific schedules relating to income property.

Part II

Real Estate Taxes
(*You can fight City Hall.*)

The only good thing about real estate taxes is that they are a deductible expense.

Real estate tax is based on the property's assessed value which in turn is based on property market value. To discourage appeals, tax authorities usually set the assessed value lower than market value. While assessed values are supposed to be based on market value, in an "up" economy, assessed values usually lag behind market value. The converse is also true. In a "down" economy, assessed values are usually higher than market values. As a taxpaying landlord, your job is to see that appraised value does not exceed the market value.

What's the difference between market value and assessed value?

Market value is what you can get for your property at any given time. A house has a different market value in summer than winter. A house with window shutters has a different market value than a similar house without shutters. Tenant-occupied property usually has a lower market value than owner-occupied property.

Too often, there is no consideration of the fact that property is tenant-occupied. Tax assessors may insist that point is not relevant. Your job is to argue that it is relevant, especially as it affects market value. You will probably win.

Should landlords always appeal high assessments?

Normally, you strive to pay the lowest tax possible. But with property, there are exceptions.

Landlords can benefit when land and building carry high assessments. When determining sales price, a higher price can be sought when a building is appraised higher. It is not a sure-fire guarantee for a higher price, but it is another independent confirming source of property value.

Conversely, when property carries a low assessed value, it is harder to justify a high sales price. If your strategy is to sell the property in a year or two, it may pay to accept a higher assessment. You pay extra taxes for the short period you own the property, but the higher assessed tax value contributes toward a higher selling price. If you don't immediately plan to sell the property, over assessments should be challenged because extra taxes cut into profits.

Special assessments

Occasionally, property owners receive special assessment notices. These one-time charges cover the cost of paving sidewalks and alleyways or other major improvements.

> *Note*: Special assessments that improve the property value are not deductible as taxes. They are capital improvements added to the property's cost basis. However, special assessments levied for *municipal* improvements are deductible as property taxes.

Some landlords purposely avoid paying the city's bill until property is sold. While the city imposes a lien against the property and interest accrues, disciplined landlords reason they can use the money more productively elsewhere on other investments. Where landlords don't have money to pay for special assessments, going the "delinquent" route means they don't have to exhaust their borrowing power to come up with funds, and they can delay payment until the property is sold.

> *Note*: This practice is not for the faint of heart and cannot go on forever. You must stay on top of dates because there is a risk that after a period of time the property will be sold at auction.

Three tax notes are in order here.

—Don't rush to pay property taxes when due, especially when municipality late charges are less than the cost of borrowing money. Interest on overdue taxes qualifies as itemized interest deductions, although penalties are not deductible.

—Don't forget to list prepaid taxes, as well as prepaid insurance as assets on bank applications. Sometimes, this can tip the scales in your favor.

—Don't forget to include on your tax return prepaid real estate taxes that appear on the settlement sheet. This is an easy mistake to make, especially since there is no tax bill for the fraction of the year, and the settlement sheet is the only place that contains this information. During the first calendar year you own a house, you will be paying more than twelve months' taxes.

Example: Mary buys a house on March 1 in a jurisdiction whose tax year begins July 1. The title company deducts four months' real estate taxes from Mary's settlement sheet to reimburse the seller. On July 1, Mary prepays her taxes for the coming year. At tax time, Mary should include the July 1 payment *and* the four months' taxes taken at settlement.

Caution: There is a flip side to this scenario for mid-year *sellers* who are reimbursed by buyers. It may be tempting to forget to offset buyer's tax reimbursement, but it is an easy error for the IRS to catch.

Challenging the city assessor/appraiser

While tax rates are set by local governments, i.e., how much per thousand, the property's assessed value is set by city appraisers ("assessors" and "appraisers" are used interchangeably). Appraisers look at a property from three different angles.

—*Age, size, design, cost, and replacement value.* Make sure the appraiser recognizes that tenant-occupied property has more wear and tear than owner-occupied property.

—*Market value.* Appraisers try to establish the property's market value based on recent sales for comparable property in your location. If there are no recent sales, they estimate the price a reasonable buyer and seller would come to. Make sure the appraiser recognizes that your property is tenant-occupied and does not compare it with the sales of owner-occupied property.

Note: In some jurisdictions, where there are no recent sales, appraisers consider what the property would sell for at a forced or distress sale such as an auction.

—*Income potential.* Make sure the appraiser recognizes not only the monthly income, but the vacancy rate and any extraordinary rental expenses you may have.

Review the appraiser's work papers.

You are entitled to review the appraiser's work papers and go over omissions and differences. Was the correct property assessed? Is the property age and description correct? Do the boundaries match the boundary descriptions contained in your deed?

Can you meet the appraiser? Yes. His or her initials are usually on the assessment worksheet. Did the appraiser actually view the property from the outside? (Assessments are sometimes made by assessors who have never even *seen* the property.) Did someone actually go *into* the property? Does the house actually contain the items contained in the appraiser's report, i.e., fireplace, number of bathrooms, etc.?

City records will show what houses on the block actually sold for. Now is the time to explain why certain houses sold for higher amounts.

The initial meeting: ten do's and don'ts

1) Bring photographs to substantiate your claim. Be prepared to leave them behind. The appraiser or reviewing official may need to attach your photographs with the case.

2) Get the appraiser to lighten up. Perhaps there is an upcoming sports event or some object on the appraiser's wall you can tastefully comment on.

3) Bring a friend to the meeting, preferably a fellow landlord. Meetings can be intimidating. A friend provides moral support and can help bolster your arguments.

4) Mentally switch hats. Play the role of appraiser to see things from his perspective.

5) Take a long time at the meeting. Let the assessor be interrupted

by phone calls and other intrusions while you "obligingly" sit waiting.

6) Bring an "expert" to the meeting. Does the property have an acute water problem or other major defect? Your "expert" can be a local repair person. If the expert cannot come in person, submit the expert's statement. Your job at administrative hearings is to introduce something "new" so that a reviewing official can justify reversing the initial determination without anyone losing face.

7) Be flexible. Be prepared to concede some points so that everyone can win something.

8) Don't plead poverty. It's not relevant to the appraisal. It is also a turn-off to the appraiser or reviewing official who is a municipal employee with possibly fewer assets than you.

9) Don't bring a tape recorder to the meeting. While some experts advise this, tape recorders put everyone on edge.

10) Don't volunteer information. The appraiser most probably has not been at the property and only has a bare description before him. Don't volunteer information about improvements you or your neighbors have made on the block. If the property is vacant, tell him. Unless asked, don't volunteer rental information prejudicial to your case.

Arguments that will lose

Reviewing officials at every level of a tax appeal are like traffic court judges. They have heard every possible excuse and scenario.

First time appellants notoriously argue non-relevant points at tax-review sessions. Don't waste everyone's time arguing that:

— taxes are too high
— there is too much government bureaucracy
— you can't afford to pay taxes
— there is too much government waste
— everyone is trying to soak you for more money
— the price you paid is less than the assessed value (In some jurisdictions this is a good argument.)
— the assessed value is greater than the insured value. (This *may* be a good argument id the insurance company sets the insured value.)

Time is on your side.

Don't rush to close a case. Once the case is open, it is in the government's interest to close the case. Even if you have a losing case, be prepared to go to court. It's another chance to settle. In fact, every stage of the appeal process provides you with another shot at settling in your favor.

Win-win solution

If you are not personally going to argue your assessment appeal, you will need a lawyer. Lawyers charge one of two ways: contingency fee, where they take a percentage of the judgment or settlement amount, or hourly rates.

Unless your appeal involves large sums of money, i.e., a large apartment complex or a shopping center, lawyers' hourly rates can be prohibitive. Smart owners find lawyers who take tax appeals on a contingency basis, i.e., the owner rebates a certain percent of the tax savings. For property owners who can't otherwise afford to pursue their claims, this is a win-win situation for lawyers and owners.

CHAPTER 11

REPAIRS

The landlord's repair obligation is surprisingly recent. Under Common Law, landlords rented only the premises, and tenants were charged with upkeep. Only during the past few decades have courts and municipalities begun to impose repair responsibility on residential property landlords. Common Law remains basically unchanged for commercial property.

Should you let tenants make repairs?

Despite good reasons for not allowing tenants to do their own repairs, most landlords encourage tenant repairs. Experts believe tenants can perform approximately 70 percent of repairs with little or no training.

There are two reasons for *not* allowing tenants to do their own repairs:

—Tenants, however well-meaning, are not usually competent.

—It is hard to raise rent when tenants make their own repairs. It may be cheaper for landlords to have outsiders do repairs and impose regular scheduled rent increases.

However, landlords encourage tenant repairs because there are few out-of-pocket expenses. There is also hope that tenants doing their own work will do a good job.

As with licensing discussed below, there is a fine line. Using a medical analogy, you wouldn't let a layman perform brain surgery, but you might allow him to pull a splinter.

The average person can do a fair percentage of repairs competently with basic tools. Yes, an element of risk and judgment is involved every time you let a tenant perform a repair. Tenants can inadvertently cause more harm than good, and if accidents ensue, there are all sorts of legal ramifications.

Your job is to minimize risk. For example, fewer things can go wrong letting tenants paint than letting tenants do plumbing or electrical work. As landlord, you have to use a certain degree of common sense and recognize that there are always certain risks. If you are not prepared to accept risk, put your money in United States savings bonds; landlording is not for you.

Must you use licensed repair people?

If local jurisdictions mandate that only licensed workmen handle certain work, there is no discussion. You must use licensed workmen. This book cannot advise otherwise. Laws requiring licensed workmen do in a way protect you. If something goes wrong with an unlicensed person's work, i.e., an electrical fire ensues, all sorts of insurance and negligence complications arise if it is discovered that work was done by unlicensed labor.

A licensed repairperson's guaranty is often better than an unlicensed worker's. Licensed people have better track records for not walking off jobs. Licensed workers have better records reporting their wages which can be important if your own tax records are ever challenged. That is not to say all unlicensed people work "off the books," but many do, and that can be a problem.

Why do people use unlicensed workers? Generally, they're cheaper. They're available. Sometimes the job is simple and routine. It's a risk many homeowners and landlords take. It is hard to fault people for trying to cut corners. It is very easy to Monday morning quarterback when something goes wrong and tell people what they *should* have done.

Dollar repair requirements

As discussed in chapter four, some landlords impose dollar repair requirements where tenants are responsible for the first $25, $40, or $50 of the repair bill and for calling the repairperson.

Landlords impose this requirement on dwellings that are in good condition. Landlords reason that the dwelling is being rented in sound shape and with all systems functioning. If toilets become clogged or window panes break, it is tenant's fault. Landlords also impose this requirement when rent is considerably below market rate. Landlords willingly accept lower rent in exchange for tenants being responsible for their own repairs.

There are advantages and disadvantages to dollar repair requirements.

Advantages of dollar repair requirements
—Tenants think twice before calling landlord for minor repairs.
—Tenants are responsible for calling repair people, being home for repairs, and seeing that repairs are correctly made.

Disadvantages of dollar repair requirements
—Tenants may try to do the repair themselves to save money and may do it incompetently.
—Tenants may defer calling for repairs, and repair jobs may become more complicated and costly.
—Too much ambiguity exists, i.e., does the dollar repair requirement extend to fixtures beyond the tenant's control, for example, roof, furnace, or hot water heater?

Some landlords handle dollar repair requirements on a case by case basis. Landlords keep the requirement in the lease and learn to trust some tenants to oversee repairs, but others, not. Landlords learn to distinguish repairs that are truly tenant's responsibility and repairs that are not.

Do tenants really destroy property?
Exaggerated horror stories of tenant destruction scare people from becoming landlords. The great majority of tenants are honest, law-abiding citizens. Think of yourself when you were renting. Tenants obviously do not treat property as carefully as owners would. You will have an unusually large occurrence of stopped toilets and clogged drains. Doorknobs will be allowed to bang into walls. But there is a difference between property neglect and willful destruction.

Items under tenant control do not last as long as they might under a landlord's control. These include locks, windows, molding, appliances, etc. These are replaceable, repairable items, and their accelerated depreciation must be considered when setting rental price.

Should tenants have your home phone number?
A school of thought exists that landlords should minimize tenant telephone accessibility. This is based on the premise that tenants can solve many problems themselves, as indeed they should. These problems include clogged drains and dealing with noisy neighbors. If the landlord is hard to reach, tenants will unclog drains themselves and

otherwise work out peaceful arrangements with their neighbors. As for major emergencies, such as fires, tenants should call the fire department first. This school of thought holds that just about all tenant communication can be in writing or to one telephone number during normal business hours.

While there is logic to this approach, as landlord you want to be on top of matters. You don't want to learn about matters affecting your property via first class mail.

Do tenants call at all hours of the night?

Tenants are no worse than some of your personal friends who also have to be trained and cajoled into earlier calling spots. Set rules. Don't be embarrassed to say, "I'm sorry, it is late, can we discuss this in the morning?"

Who is an employee?

Over the course of landlording, you will be hiring many different people to do things for you. You may view service people as *independent contractors*; others may view them as common law *employees*. More than semantics are involved.

Workers are classified as "employees" if you, the employer, control the results of the work and the means and methods of accomplishing that result.

For employees, you are responsible for withholding taxes, FICA, Medicare, unemployment insurance, and workman's compensation. There can be a whole host of other fringe benefits, assorted reporting requirements, and rules and regulations that you must be aware of.

You can understand why landlords prefer to consider workers independent contractors responsible for their own taxes and benefits. Conversely, you can understand why the IRS and local government often take the opposite view. If the IRS classifies your "independent contractor" an "employee," you can be liable for back withholding taxes, penalties, interest, etc.

Independent contractors

To successfully claim workers as independent contractors:
   —Workers should offer their services to the general public, in occupations traditionally accepted as independent contractors, for example, plumbers, painters, electricians. It helps if workers work

for several people simultaneously, although the IRS has recognized situations where independent contractors work primarily for one employer.

—Workers provide their own tools, equipment, or workplace.

—Workers can incur a loss as a result of their work.

—Workers are trained and do not need special training or supervision.

—Workers are responsible only for getting a specific job done, i.e., it helps if they come and go as they please, they do not keep set hours, and can delegate work to others.

—Workers control how they do the job, i.e., you the landlord do not control the means and methods. A worker can quit whenever he wants.

Note: You are responsible for reporting to the IRS, fees (in excess of a threshold amount, i.e., $600) tendered to independent contractors (Form 1096). You must also submit a Form 1099 to the independent contractor by February 1. Besides being the law, this protects you at audit time, i.e., you can substantiate your expenses.

Some experts advise getting indemnification letters from workers. attesting to their independent contractor status, and that they will reimburse you if their status is determined to be that of an employee.

Other experts recommend the opposite; *don't* get the letter, because the existence of such a letter means that there was justifiable doubt on your part.

Note: Consider "leased labor" which is becoming ever more popular. Leased labor is a hybrid combination of independent contractors and employees. Employee-leasing agencies supply you with workers. You pay one check to the agency, and they are responsible for payroll, withholding, benefits, deductions, rules, regulations, reporting, etc.

Working with contractors and repairmen

Normally, no special charm is needed. Your repair call should be promptly and courteously handled. But, as a homeowner and a landlord, you know that is not the case. Contractors and repair people sometimes fail to show up, or show up days later. They leave work in the middle while rushing off to other jobs. They ask for greater advances than they are entitled.

Before faulting servicemen, make sure your own behavior is in order.

—Are you courteous to them?

—Do you pay your bills on time?

—Do you stand over them too much?

—Are you super critical?

—Are you constantly changing your mind?

—Do you tell them how to do their job?

—Do you demand extras "thrown in"?

—Do you provide decent working conditions?

Repair people will tell you all sorts of horror stories to explain why they walked off a job or why they don't respond to certain individuals' phone calls. Only if *your* behavior is in order, can you use "Dale Carnegie" on others.

Contractors and service people must be charmed. It is your job to inspire their creativity and motivation to complete the job. Feel free to use whatever it takes.

—*Cookies, drinks, and food.* Workmen usually disappear midday in search of food or coffee. If the job is important, consider providing food and drinks.

—*Compliments.* Compliments work, especially if they are sincere.

—*Teamwork.* If you are competent, inclined, and welcomed, sometimes servicemen can use a hand.

—*Enthusiasm and purpose.* Workmen appreciate noble causes and realistic deadlines.

Keep the job simple.

In grocery stores, savings are usually realized by buying a larger size. This is *not* true in the repair and contracting business. Big jobs cost *more* than small, piecemeal jobs.

Let's take for example finishing a tenant's basement. A contractor gives an estimate based on his subcontracting of work which may include masonry, carpentry, plumbing, electrical work, plastering, and paneling. The contractor's estimate includes provisions for labor and material overruns for each category. Because the contractor is dealing with subcontractors with whom he has less control, if the contractor errs, he has to err on the side of caution, i.e., charge you more.

An alternative for the landlord seeking the best job at the best price is to divide the work into smaller jobs. A plumber does plumbing, a carpenter does carpentry, etc. Besides cutting out the contractor-middleman, each worker is responsible for his own labor and material and can give a better price. Obviously, this requires more landlord involvement than just assigning the project to a contractor; however, the savings can make it worthwhile.

Repair or replace?

This issue confronts owners of expensive items from cars to television sets. While there is no right or wrong answer, you feel like a fool spending $100 to fix a $250 television that soon dies.

The good thing about investment property is that there are positive tax aspects for repairs and installing new equipment. If you have been careful to escrow money for major repairs, the financial pain of big ticket items is lessened. You are not spending your money—you are spending escrowed money.

Don't forget the cost of capital consideration

Example: Let's say a new roof for rental property is $3,000 and your cost of capital, the commercial interest rate to borrow this money, is 12 percent. This comes to $360 a year in simple interest. If it doesn't cost you more than $360 a year to fix the roof, you may be better off just patching the roof every year.

Tenants want to be loved.

Another reason to repair and not replace is that tenants like to see you making repairs on their behalf. Repairs on behalf of tenants is a landlord's way of showing love. It also helps justify rent increases and gives you a reason to turn down other requests, i.e., because you just spent $360 this month for the roof, the tenant will have to make due with the existing dishwasher.

Brand names

Contractors will try to convince you to go for brand-name appliances and better quality materials. While no one really cares what kind of interior studs you use, it's okay to go top-of-the- line for items that become selling or renting points, i.e., a frost-free refrigerator instead of a regular one; a brand name ceiling fan instead of a cheap import. Needless to say, the higher the rent the more that is expected in terms of quality and brand names.

Contracts: Do you need them?

No sane person can advise you to initiate work without a contract. In real life, however, landlords and contractors often work with handshake agreements. Landlords reason that, if the contractor or workman is a "fly-by-night," the contract is not worth the paper it is written on anyway. Landlords often assume the element of risk of working without a contract, especially if trust has built up over the years.

A half way position is to write down the job specifications, even if it is not a formal contract. While perhaps not enforceable, the parties between themselves know what is expected, i.e., a 75,000 BTU furnace is to be installed, not a 50,000 BTU furnace.

Advances

Experts unanimously and in the strongest terms caution against advances to contractors and workmen beyond the initial down payment or scheduled payment.

That said, every landlord, including the toughest, at some point mistakenly succumbed to workmen's pleas and prematurely advanced funds.

For the uninitiated, the problem with advancing funds is that once funds are advanced the workman has little incentive to finish the job or finish the job properly. Contractors often use funds from one project to complete other projects. When it comes time to finish your project, funds were already spent and funds from yet another project are required.

Advance planning by landlords is required.
—Before signing a contract, landlords should emphatically state that there is only one rule they solidly enforce, the rule against premature advances. Said convincingly, the contractor will go to others for advances.
—Landlords should not assume a well-off monied position, i.e., that they even have excess money to advance. Let the contractor know how many tenants are behind in their rent and financial woes

affecting you.

—Good guy/bad guy approach. Here the landlord plays the good guy. "I would love to advance money, but the bank (bad guy) or my partner or husband (bad guy) will not let me."

Good records

If you're going to make it in the landlording business, you must learn to keep good records. With good records you will learn the various life spans of appliances. You will be able to predict when items need replacement. As you can imagine, appliances used by tenants have shorter life spans than appliances used by landlords. With good records you may find your management company charging you twice for the same items. Confront the company. They may claim honest error, but they now know you *read* bills. Confront the company if you find yourself paying for an item that was just fixed. Perhaps the company can get an adjustment from the repairperson. If you don't raise the issue, no one else will.

Know your property.

If the property has gas heat, raise Cain if you find yourself billed for an *oil* furnace contract or repair. If your property has circuit breakers, why were you charged for fuses? Errors like this happen more often than you think.

Know the law.

If your local jurisdiction does not require landlords of single-family houses to rid a house of infestation, you may wish to challenge extermination bills. If local jurisdictions require *tenants* to keep single-family yards clean, you should find no yard clean-up bills imposed on the landlord.

Beware of sweetheart deals.

Beware of a repairperson whose brother-in-law is in a related repair business. Two examples suffice.

Example 1: The painter you carefully selected notices water spots on the ceiling and obligingly tells you his friend, brother-in-law, or neighbor, etc. is in the roofing business. You may find yourself springing for a new roof by a less than competent person.

Example 2: Your air-conditioning repairman also does heating repairs. The repairman fixes the air-conditioning unit in the summer and removes a wire from the heating unit. In mid-fall, your tenant turns on the heat and it doesn't work. You call the repairman who surprisingly knows exactly what to do.

No one will ever know the dollar amount of unnecessary repairs done in this country. You can minimize the chances of being victim by making it a strict policy to separate repair responsibilities. In the above example, the air-conditioning repairman would have no incentive to remove a heating wire if he knew you used a different person for heating repairs.

Special assessments and municipal repairs

Periodically, you will receive notice that the sidewalk in front of your rental house is cracked, or the curb or public alley is in disrepair.

Municipalities sometimes allow you to select your own contractor. For small jobs, this is more tease than choice. Your contractor has to submit plans to the city, obtain permits, and post various bonds. Generally, city contractors are competitive with any contractor you will select, especially for small jobs.

> *Note*: Don't expect *quick* city action. The good thing about government is it frequently falls behind processing special assessments. It can take the city months after the notice to award the contract to a successful bidder, months for the bidder to complete the work, months for the city to inspect the work, and months thereafter for the city to bill you. Sometimes, work orders just get lost in the system, and the matter is essentially dropped.

Beware of tenant jealousy.

When tenants know each other, as they will in multi-unit and two-family houses, repairs and improvements made for one tenant are expected by other tenants.

I recall one incident where owners of a fancy garden apartment complex decided to replace regular kitchen tile with new no-wax kitchen floors in *some* apartments. Tenants in the apartments where new floors were *not* laid became jealous and put pots of boiling water on the floors to bring up the old tile. These tenants were otherwise fine and upstanding citizens, but unfortunately felt they had to destroy property to get what their neighbors received.

Lastly, beware of the first year.

Another rule of thumb for new landlords is that repair costs are the highest during your first year of ownership. The former owner, knowing of the impending property sale, most likely neglected to make certain repairs. Accordingly, you can expect your highest repair costs during your first year.

A Murphy's type law which is true for both new landlords and new homeowners is that *a house knows when there are new owners.*

A furnace that was intact for twenty years will fail on the second week of your ownership. A roof that never needed repairs will leak on the third week. Every homeowner and landlord can relate similar stories. The only thing you can do is prepare. You must have a nest egg for these "unexpected" emergencies. If you don't, you may wish to reconsider your plans.

CHAPTER 12

PROBLEMS AND SOLUTIONS

— *Accidents*
— *Fire*
— *Discrimination*
— *Hazardous materials*
— *Fences and adverse possession*

I. Accidents

Accidents happen. As hard as you try to maintain your property, accidents happen. And when accidents happen, tenants blame landlords.

Damage Control. Some landlords try placating tenants. For example, if a tenant got sick because the furnace broke over the weekend leaving the tenant without heat, the landlord brings tenant hot, homemade soup. If a tenant injures himself falling down the steps, the landlord visits with a bouquet of flowers.

Naive? Maybe. But some landlords do very well with damage control. Sometimes, sincere courtesy is all that is needed: "I'm sorry you fell, I hope this makes you feel better."

Some landlords throw more in as incentive: "I'm sorry the washing machine flooded your basement. Can I rebate a half-month's rent for your inconvenience?" In this day and age of lawsuits, some landlords do very well with this approach.

For some tenants, a landlord's apology and offer of help is sufficient. Tenants understand that accidents happen. They just do not want to be taken for granted.

Note: There is an art to appeasement. Don't say, as above, "I'm sorry about what happened. Can I rebate a half-month's rent?" The tenant thinks if this is what the landlord is offering, the landlord must really fear a higher figure will be sought. Savvy tenants will ask for more.

Rather say, "I'm sorry about what happened. What can I do to help?" The tenant is overwhelmed by your offer. Since in the back of his mind he may have thought he would get nothing, his expectations might be totally lower than your offer. His request may even be minimal.

A small minority of landlords hold the opposite position. They say, *never say you're sorry*. It is a show of weakness. For many of these landlords, the approach, ironically, works. Many tenants are intimidated from pursuing a claim.

Lawsuits

For a small group of tenants, neither a nice approach nor hard-nosed approach works. These are suers, also known as "suitcases," who sue for both real and imaginary hurts. How should you respond?

Stay cool. Tenant wrath is not directed at you personally, but rather at your insurance company.

Dealing with your insurance company

Do you have to inform your insurance company of a possible claim? Unfortunately, the answer is yes. That requirement is also buried in the lines of print that come with your insurance policy. But look at it from the insurance company's view. Most jurisdictions give a plaintiff two or three years to bring suit. If a plaintiff brings suit a year and a half after the accident, an insurance company can rightfully claim it is nearly impossible to assess the claim's validity. Had the company been apprised of the possible claim when the accident occurred, it could have investigated the matter while the facts were fresh. Whether you agree with that argument, that is the basis for insurance companies denying claims made long after an investigation is feasible.

At what point do you have to inform your insurance company of a possible claim? Probably when a tenant tells you point-blank he's going to see a lawyer.

Addressing the question of when must a landlord notify his insurance company of a possible claim, a court in my state ruled responsibility is imposed when "an accident is sufficiently serious to lead a person of ordinary intelligence and prudence to believe that it might give rise to a claim for damages."

Obviously, no landlord wants to see frivolous claims rewarded. Claims impact on premiums and insurability. But you are not the insurance company's investigator or trier of fact. You are not a detective.

Keep notes because the insurance company will contact you for your version of the incident, and where possible get photographs.

> *Note*: Photographs can work against you, i.e., in a litigated proceeding, opposing counsel can order photographs produced in a deposition. With hindsight in mind, take photographs only if doing so is to your advantage.

Possible defenses
—Tenant was aware of the problem.
—Tenant aggravated the problem.
—Tenant never informed landlord of the problem.
—Tenant tried to fix the problem himself, but did so negligently.
—Tenant did not allow landlord to fix the problem.
—Tenant was drunk, stoned, etc. at time of accident.
—Landlord was in full compliance with the law.

After turning the matter over to the insurance company, forget it. Too many landlords become preoccupied with what they think the case outcome should be. As you can imagine, more often than not, insurance companies settle, and life goes on. In the words of my insurance agent, "Relax, don't let the tail wag the dog."

II. Fires
Fires are rare, but they do happen. Fire fighters break windows and doors. Gas and electric companies shut utilities off. There is smoke and water damage and lots of debris. Sometimes, adjoining properties are affected as well.

After a fire, the house most probably is no longer habitable. Under Common Law, tenants are still obligated to pay rent under the lease, but modern law takes a more "liberal" approach and requires that premises be habitable for the lease to continue.

Reports
Two reports will be made: a fire report and a police report. Make sure you get both reports. They are written from two different perspectives. They are not necessarily the same. As to the cause of the fire, they may be diametrically opposite.

> *Note*: To get these reports in larger cities, contact the city or county office of records. In other jurisdictions, these can be obtained from the police or fire department. There is usually a small charge.

Probable vs. possible cause
Police and fire investigators will attempt to determine the cause of the fire. When the cause is unknown, anything is possible, i.e., a window was open and a spark flew in.

Probable cause is supported by evidence, i.e., a severely burnt bed may indicate that the fire originated in bed.

Was it the tenant's fault?
Two possibilities exist:

1) The fire was intentionally set. Perhaps a spouse or girlfriend wanted revenge, or a teenager was engaged in an illegal activity. Perhaps a tenant wanted to collect on his insurance policy. These are *criminal* situations involving police. You may have a civil recourse against the perpetrator, but recovery is doubtful.

2) The fire was accidental. Under this category comes
— *gross negligence*, i.e., the tenant stored gasoline in the house in an improper container
— *ordinary negligence*, i.e., the tenant fell asleep while smoking in bed.
— *accident*, i.e., while cooking and exercising ordinary care, a stove fire occurred.

You might have a claim against the tenant's gross negligence, but not usually for ordinary negligence or plain accident.

Was it the landlord's fault?

Again, two possibilities exist:

1) *Criminal.* The fire was intentionally set. More than just the land-lord's direct act may be involved. The landlord's act or omission or omission may be criminal because of a statute or ordinance.

2) *Accident* because of:

—*Gross negligence,* i.e., the landlord knew of a serious problem and failed to act, or acted in a grossly negligent way.

—*Ordinary negligence,* i.e., the landlord allowed too much stuff to be kept in the storage room where the fire originated.

—*Accident,* i.e., the motor in the landlord's refrigerator caught fire.

As above, usually nothing is owed to tenants for *accidents* and *ordinary negligence.* Insurance should protect you in all three instances: gross negligence, ordinary negligence, and accidents. Obviously, the landlord will not collect if his actions were criminal.

Who gets called?

After the police and fire departments leave the scene, you must contact your insurance company. Their investigator will go to the scene to verify the fire cause and assess the scope of damage. Do not sign anything right away, because you have no way of knowing the scope of the damages.

Most often, the house needs immediate boarding because doors and windows are out. If your insurance company does not ordinarily handle this, ask them to refer you to people who do.

> *Note:* Expect to pay dearly for the work "board up" companies perform. If possible, arrange for this work privately.

Certified public adjusters

I strongly recommend obtaining the services of a certified public fire adjuster. These people work on commission, i.e., approximately 5 to 10 percent of the insurance settlement. They take care of boarding up the property and hauling away debris (at your expense) if your insurance company does not pick up the tab. They work with police, fire, and insurance investigators, and later with insurance company adjusters.

Adjusters negotiate the best possible settlement for you. They know the effect that fire, water, smoke, and odor have on every single house component and how it effects marketability. Even with their commission, they usually obtain a better settlement than you can obtain by yourself. Don't hesitate using them. Your insurance company will use the fire against you at renewal time anyway, so you might as well get the best possible settlement.

> *Note*: Public adjusters will give you repair estimates from several independent contractors on their Roladex list. Exercise caution before accepting these bids; you can probably get better bids yourself.

What if your property is damaged by the fire next door?

You can try to collect damages from your neighbor's policy. However, don't expect your neighbor to volunteer information concerning his company. And when you contact his company, don't expect their cooperation. They will maintain that they are not obligated to pay unless you can prove probable cause and fault going beyond ordinary negligence.

Your damage will probably have to be reimbursed by your own insurance company, and they in turn will try to collect from your neighbor's company. Even though the fire did not originate at your property, your company may hold this against you when determining whether to insure your property and at what rate. On small claims involving investment property, you may be better off absorbing the loss yourself, rather than facing a drastic rate boost or insurance cut off.

Absorbing losses yourself

> *Example*: Fire breaks out in the basement furnace, causing minor smoke and structural damage, and destroys the furnace.

Where damage is small and limited to the landlord's property, whether right or wrong, many landlords absorb the loss without notifying their insurance company. Landlords realize that their failure to timely notify the insurance company may cause them to be precluded from reimbursement.

Doing so, there is an element of risk that tenants might subsequently claim their property was involved or some other injury. Too, subsequent discovery might reveal that the fire did more damage than originally thought.

So why do landlords absorb minor losses? Because landlords are scared of premiums going up or being dropped by insurance companies. In the above example where fire destroys the furnace, the landlord can replace the old furnace with a new one for about $1,000 to $1,500. Considering that the average insurance policy comes with a $250 to $500 deductible, and considering too that the old furnace was probably more than just a few years old, the landlord may not do so badly absorbing the loss himself. The landlord's rating remains intact, and the property has a new furnace which is usually more efficient than the old one.

How long must you keep copies of insurance policies?

In a one-word answer—forever. Not only must you save receipts, you also must save copies of the actual policies.

Some insurance companies play the prove-it game. *You* have to prove to them you were insured! You would expect insurance companies, in this age of microfilm and computerization, to have a complete record of your coverage. They probably do, but they certainly will not admit it. Their first response is for you to submit copies (some demand originals) of all policies. They claim to need this information to determine their liability. An insured who no longer has copies of his policies, current or expired, has a difficult task ahead of him.

Let's get more extreme. While adults are limited to bringing claims within a certain statute of limitations, i.e., in some jurisdictions three years, this generally does not apply to minors. The statute of limitations for a minor bringing suit begins when the minor reaches the age of majority. Thus, if a child was two when the accident occurred, and the state age of majority is eighteen years, a claim can be brought against a landlord nineteen years after the accident!

For these reasons, keep all expired policies.

III. Discrimination

Every now and then, landlords are startled to read about landlords socked with fair housing discrimination awards. Awards and settlements can exceed six figures, and worse, there is usually no insurance to protect the landlord.

When federal laws were first enacted, there were two main exceptions. The law did not pertain to:

— single-family houses sold or rented by owners who did not own three or more single-family houses at one time. There were some limitations, i.e., the owner could not use the services of a real estate agent to facilitate the sale or rental, and the house could not be advertised in a discriminatory manner.

— dwellings with four or fewer units, providing the owner of the building lives in one of the units.

Other exceptions applied to religious organizations and private clubs that are not relevant here.

While federal law may allow certain exceptions, local laws often do not. State and local jurisdictions often impose stricter standards.

Whatever your personal or political feelings are, the simple fact remains that discrimination is against the law. Not only will civic authorities come against you with fines and jail terms, but injured plaintiffs and their lawyers will come against you as well. There seems to be no limit to the amount of punitive damages that can be awarded.

The most common form of discrimination is race discrimination. A person of one race feels he or she was excluded from a dwelling on account of race. Other forms of rental discrimination include sex, religion, color, family status or national origin.

You cannot say that a dwelling is unavailable for inspection, sale, or rent, when in fact it is available. Private and government groups sometimes send "plants," which gives an added reason to be wary.

> Note: Discrimination can be subtle. One suit was filed against a landlord who when interviewing white tenants, offered coffee but did not offer coffee to prospective black tenants.

Once discrimination charges have been leveled, the burden shifts to the landlord to prove that there was no discrimination.

Discrimination goes the other way too. Landlords are sometimes accused of placing minority tenants in properties in order to get adjacent owners to move. This may be *blockbusting*. Jurisdictions specifically prohibit blockbusting, which is subject to fine and/or imprisonment. Landlords cannot place tenants in properties with total disregard to any objective standards.

Other protected categories

Other protected discrimination categories include age, marital status, and physical or mental handicap. Included in physical handicap may be people with AIDS. Some jurisdictions extend protection to sexual orientation, (i.e., gays and lesbians) and families receiving public assistance.

Must a *devout* landlord rent to an unmarried couple? No. A recent California appeals court overturned a ruling by the California Employment and Fair Housing Commission and ruled that a *landlord's* constitutionally protected religious rights to religious freedom would be violated. The court ruled that the landlord was entitled to an exemption because of "sincere religious beliefs that fornication and its facilitation are sins." This case is being watched nationally and has broad implications, especially since it also can extend to gay couples who cannot legally marry.

Adult-only housing

Recent federal legislation has all but banned adult-only housing, limiting adult-only housing to retirement housing where special services are provided to residents and communities where residents are over sixty-two years old.

Handicapped housing

Laws for the protection of the handicapped have been enacted, covering apartment buildings built after March 1991. Public areas must be accessible. Included are provisions for lowered light switches and widened doorways. Kitchens and bathrooms have to be designed to accommodate the handicapped. Multi-family buildings built before March 1991 must provide reasonable accommodation (ramps, designated handicap parking spaces) where that can be reasonably done. Landlords must also let tenants make "reasonable modification" of the premises at tenant's expense, i.e., grab bars in bathrooms, widened doorways, etc. These laws require that premises be returned to its prior condition at the termination of the tenancy, especially when the alteration interferes with the next tenant's use of the property.

Advertising

Newspaper ads also must be discrimination-free. You do not have to advertise in minority publications, and you do not have to specifically advertise EOH (equal opportunity housing), but sometimes it helps to do both, especially if you plan to own many units.

When ads picture groups of people, the group should include members of all races. There are civic-minded people out there who actually monitor newspaper ads to bring lawsuits. In my own community, one large realty firm settled out of court and turned over a six-figure amount to pacify a civic-minded plaintiffs' organization. Conversely, another large realty firm refused to settle and prevailed in court that single-race ads by themselves, without any discriminatory practice, do not violate the Fair Housing Act.

How to keep undesirables out of your rentals

Unless you are a skinhead who would not rent to a minority person, even if he or she was a U.S. Supreme Court Justice, think about the type of person you want to exclude from your rental. As long as you apply your standards equally, you can achieve your desired results without unlawfully discriminating.

—If you want to exclude persons without adequate resources to pay rent or security deposit, that is fine. No court in the land will challenge you.

—If you want to exclude persons with unreliable rent payment histories, that is fine.

—If you want to exclude people who can't produce satisfactory references, that is also fine.

—If you want to exclude persons *convicted* of felonies, fine. (Note the use of the term "convicted." You can't just use the term "arrested," because sometimes people who are arrested are acquitted.)

—If you want to limit the number of people occupying a single residence, that is permitted too, although in most instances you cannot specifically exclude children.

Note: A landlord enforcing a one-person, one-bedroom rule, i.e., no more than three occupants in a three-bedroom house, may be sued for housing-law bias where such rule acts to deter minority family occupancy. Informal guidelines established by the United States Department of Housing and Urban Development suggest a two person per bedroom occupancy standard.

—If you want to exclude people from running businesses out of the rental property, that is permitted too.

Experts advise documenting appointments. What *else* turned you off about a particular person? Were they late, ill-mannered, slovenly? How were their references? If you are a landlord who inspects tenants' prior residence, was it neat? Again, once a discrimination charge is leveled, the burden is on you. But with proper documentation, you can prevail.

However, as careful and as non-arbitrary as you try to be, the bare results sometimes work against you. If you have scores of units, and not one of them over a period of time is rented to a minority person, there is a presumption of discrimination that you may otherwise have to rebut. The only remedy is to develop your own form of affirmative action or show that at least you tried.

IV. Hazardous materials: The good news

Nothing scares landlords more than toxic hazards horror stories: retardation, death, lawsuits, settlements, judgments, and insurance companies excluding toxic hazards from coverage.

What are toxic hazards?

The list keeps growing: asbestos found in insulation; radon gas leakage; carbon monoxide; microwave radiation leakage; formaldehyde in the air; pollutants in drinking water; dust mites and chemicals in carpeting; lead-contaminated soil; electromagnetic fields, etc.

If you want something additional to worry about, you can now worry about garden vegetable patches framed with pressure-treated wood, backyard decks, and playground equipment. Pressure-treated wood is saturated with chemicals toxic to fungi and insects that cause wood to decompose. These same chemicals (chromium, copper, and arsenic) have been classified as human carcinogens. You can also worry about kitchen cabinets and counter tops that have a particleboard core. Glue in particleboard contains formaldehyde, a colorless gas that is released into the home environment. I have not yet heard of any pressure-treated wood or particleboard lawsuits, but give plaintiffs' lawyers a chance.

The good news. I don't mean to belittle toxic hazards, but there is so much scary literature out there, you do not need another section here devoted to landlord horror stories.

So we are going to do something different—something popular magazines don't publish. We're going to discuss the *good* news about pollutants, starting with lead paint.

The good news about lead paint is that it is an immense national problem. Most homes built before 1977 contain lead paint—*some 20 million American homes*; I've seen one figure claiming *57 million American homes*, more than half the nation's housing stock! Danger from lead paint has been known since 1978 when lead was finally banned from paints, and probably many years before that.

The good news for landlords is that the problem is so monstrously big, that it is not just a landlord's problem. How big? One group has estimated lead removal at more than *$240 billion dollars*, and that figure is just for 24 million homes and apartments where it is most needed.

The federal government cannot effectively eliminate the problem because the federal government is one of the biggest owners of lead-based homes. The Department of Housing and Urban Development alone subsidizes 4.5 million units, many of which are lead-based. State and municipal governments own thousands of lead-based houses, schools, hospitals, etc. And lead poisoning does not only come from paint. It comes from pottery and china plates, dust inside buildings, and dust kicked up by incineration and municipal drinking water as well. While the EPA tightened drinking water standards for lead in May, 1991, it gave utility companies up to twenty years to comply!

My own community recently terminated its lead-removal program because the city solicitor advised that the city could face a subsequent lawsuit if children living in a house treated by the city subsequently came down with lead poisoning.

If millions of homes are involved, exposing millions of children since at least 1978, there should be thousands and thousands of decided cases holding landlords liable for this terrible plague.

Spend an afternoon in a law library and you will actually find very few decided lead paint cases. And now the good news:

The cases go largely in the landlord's favor!

Courts have held that lead-paint is not a "concealed dangerous condition," i.e., tenants have the same knowledge as landlords as to the age of the house and the likelihood for lead paint. Courts have held that the possibility of children eating paint chips is "not foreseeable," and that parents are contributory negligent for not watching their children. Courts have held for landlords who even painted with lead paint. Courts have held that landlords must have actual notice of the contamination. Obviously, if a landlord conceals the condition, or falsely represents to a tenant that a house is lead-free, there can be an action against the landlord for misrepresentation.

More good news. Courts have held insurance companies responsible for defending toxic pollutant cases. One case in particular involved a tenant allergic to urea-formaldehyde foam insulation. The court held that the defense of the suit came under the insured's liability policy, covering "bodily injury." There do not appear to be many decided cases where insurance companies tried to escape responsibility defending lead poisoning cases. I suspect these cases settle without going to trial.

Insurance companies of late have been modifying policies to exclude toxic materials such as asbestos and lead paint. Again, there are not many test cases. Should the practice become universal, plaintiffs' lawyers will have to reassess their strategies, especially since landlords are beginning to use state- of-the-art legal arrangements to protect their assets from judgments.

Landlords should not stay aloof from this national (international?) calamity, but neither should they be expected to single-handedly bear the costs of remedying toxic pollution.

V. Fences

Fences become problems when an adjoining property owner installs a boundary fence and wants you to chip in, or conversely, if you install a fence on your property and you want your neighbor to pay for part of it.

Your gut reaction might be that if the local jurisdiction does not require fences (these laws are called fence statutes) and you wish to install one on your property, you have to do so at your own expense.

Surprisingly, court decisions go the other way, and will require a neighbor to chip in for a fence that both neighbors use. The request must be reasonable, i.e., a court may hesitate requiring an equal sharing of costs if the fence is overly elaborate. Courts will also require both neighbors to chip in for fence maintenance.

Example: Landlord's property lies between two properties that have boundary fences. Landlord constructs a fence on the third side of landlord's yard, thereby fully enclosing the landlord's property. Most jurisdictions will require landlord to chip in to the other two owners since the landlord is benefiting and making use of their fences.

Adverse possession

Problems sometimes arise when a neighbor installs a fence on your property or there is some other encroachment on your property. The situation of course could be the other way around, if your shed is partially on your neighbor's lot.

Most jurisdictions provide that, if encroachment has existed for a certain number of years, i.e., five to twenty-one years, property rights revert to the encroacher! A few conditions must be met. Encroachment must be adverse, i.e., it cannot be with your neighbor's permission. It must also be actual, continuous, open, and exclusive.

Note: To protect your property rights from being lost to adverse possession, send a letter to your "encroaching" neighbor, saying that you understand that your neighbor's garage extends on your property, but that you give your neighbor permission for the encroachment, and that your permission should not be construed as a gift of property. If you don't want to give permission, you may sue to have the garage removed from your property.

CHAPTER 13

ZONING

Can government tell you what to do?

Zoning is using your property as permitted by law. It applies both to interior use, i.e., operating a business in a residential dwelling, and to exterior use, i.e., setbacks, additions, and building heights.

Zoning is upheld where public welfare and interest is involved. The Constitution grants government the right to regulate land use to protect the health, morals, and welfare of its citizens.

Check the zoning.

Too often, first time buyers assume property is lawfully zoned for the use being sold. Later, they find that the purchased two-family dwelling is in a single-family district or the property they bought to rent as a business is not zoned for business.

Don't accept the real estate agent's zoning *belief* as the final word. Experience teaches to call the zoning office to verify the zoning status and, where great sums of money are involved, to get the zoning status in writing.

See if there is any planned future use that will impact negatively on your property. For example, has that nearby adjacent lot been approved for a freeway or a school for incorrigible youth?

Caution: When checking at the zoning office, don't volunteer property information to the "friendly" zoning clerk. It can be used against you.

Real-life example: Bob K. considered purchasing a two-family house in a single-family area. A call to the zoning office confirmed the dwelling was authorized to house two families. The "friendly" clerk asked Bob if the house was vacant. Bob answered yes and volunteered that the house was vacant in excess of a year. That was a big mistake.

Under the rules of that particular jurisdiction, since two-family houses were excepted uses "grandfathered" in, their status reverted back to single-family use if the excepted use (two-family dwelling) was not continuously used as a two-family dwelling. "Continuous" in that jurisdiction meant that the dwelling could not be vacant for more than a year. The "friendly" clerk felt duty-bound to alert her supervisor who terminated the non-conforming excepted use.

Grandfathering

In zoning language, "grandfathering" is a permitted exception to zoning rules based on prior use, i.e., if the use was allowed during "grandfather's" time, the use is permitted now.

Common examples are residential neighborhood gas stations and corner grocery stores. Often, these businesses predate residential development or zoning laws. Today, after the neighborhood is residential, a new gas station or grocery store might not be permitted, but zoning authorities sometimes allow "grandfathered" businesses to continue.

Landlords often will find this with single-family houses that were subdivided many years ago before current zoning rules. Current zoning might not allow subdividing, but it often permits earlier subdivided houses to continue as subdivided houses.

However, just because a house is zoned for two families or was "grandfathered in" does not mean it complies with necessary building codes, especially relating to room size, parking spaces, fire-prevention requirements, handicap accessibility, etc.

Grandfathering is not an absolute protection. In some instances, "grandfathering" allows exemption from current building and zoning codes, in some cases not. For example, current building codes require bathrooms to be so many square feet. Bathrooms in many older buildings fall below current requirements. Nevertheless, "grandfathering" permits older bathrooms to be used without a change in room size.

> Note: Grandfathered immunity can be lost when "substantial" renovation is performed, i.e., when more than 50 percent of the property is being renovated. In the above example, if more

than 50 percent of the property is being renovated, a renovated bathroom may have to meet current square footage requirements. If this is a problem, potential rehabbers may wish to consider renovating in stages.

Immunity can be lifted. For example, just because a billboard on the side of a house was previously permitted does not mean it is allowed now. Some billboard removal laws are absolute, i.e., they do not recognize grandfathering, and the billboard must come down. Others are time-factored, i.e., no new billboards after a certain date. Can a municipality do this? Sure. Zoning is not forever - zoning laws constantly change.

When laws change

Case 1: Sarah rents Donna a house for use as a residence and a daycare center. Zoning laws subsequently prohibit home day-care centers. Donna wants to be released from the lease and wants her security deposit back.

Courts generally favor the landlord. Here, Donna can still use the leasehold as a residence, even though zoning regulations restrict use of *part* of the premises.

Variations of this arise where zoning laws subsequently restrict the number of people who can be employed in a home business. Since zoning effects only part of the use, the tenant is still bound to the lease.

Case 2: Ron rents Dr. Vision, an eye doctor, a house for office use. Unknown to Ron and Dr. Vision, offices are not permitted in the particular residential area. Dr. Vision wants to be released from the lease and wants his security deposit back.

Here, courts generally favor the tenant. The lease for an office in a residential areas was illegal *from the start*. Courts will not enforce void and illegal contracts. If Dr. Vision is required only to obtain a license or permit to conduct business, some courts require him to do so. Some courts hold that, where zoning boards have authority to hear appeals, Dr. Vision must exhaust this remedy to be released from the lease.

Converting a single-unit dwelling to a two-unit dwelling

Landlords like to increase the number of rental units on a given property. Landlords reason that income increases while most expenses remain the same, i.e., there is only one roof, basement, etc. to maintain.

However, landlords should think twice. Increasing a single-family house to a two-family house is not always recommended.

—Single-family houses have value to other investors and to home owners. In many areas of the country, the resale market for two-unit dwellings is rather limited.

—Dividing a single-family house into two units, halves the living space and limits use. Problems arise between tenants concerning basement, front and rear yards, driveway, etc.

—Single-family dwellings are more often inhabited by families. Landlords will confirm that families move less frequently than single people or childless couples who would most likely occupy your two-unit dwelling.

   Note: In some areas of the country where housing is tight, two-unit dwellings may be the norm for families with children.

—Converted two-family dwellings often do not have adequate soundproofing for walls and floors. These are prime areas for tenant discontent.

—Utilities are usually borne by the occupant of a single-family dwelling. Unless the owner installs separate hot water heaters, furnaces, electric and gas lines, the *owner* pays utilities. In the past, landlords complained about high energy bills only during the winter. Today, when almost everyone relies on air-conditioning, energy bills can be devastating May through September as well as during the November to March heating months.

—Ditto for water bills. On single dwellings, tenants pay water bills. Most jurisdictions do not allow separate water meters for two-unit dwellings, and these now become the *landlord's* responsibility. *Note*: Some jurisdictions prohibit landlords from splitting the water bill between the tenants.

—Renters of single-family dwellings are responsible for their yards, trash, and snow removal. Once a dwelling houses two families, responsibility for who does what gets messy.

Can a tenant subdivide a dwelling into two units?

If your lease prohibits subletting, this should not be a problem. A tenant violating the subletting clause can be evicted.

Some landlords, however, do not particularly care if another family occupies a portion of the rented house as long as rent is timely paid. This is especially true when times are tough and subletting is the only way tenants can afford to stay.

Where not restricted by lease, courts generally allow tenants to sublet a portion of the house to another when the second rental is *incidental* to the overall house usage.

Case 1: A widow renting a house in a single-family zoning district sublets the basement to another family. The jurisdiction sues under the single-family zoning provision. At trial, the Court allows the basement rental because it is *incidental* to the overall rental.

Case 2: A divorced parent keeps one room of a rented house for himself and rents the rest of the dwelling to another family. The jurisdiction sues under the single-family zoning provision. At trial, the court disallows the second rental which is not incidental to the overall rental but rather is the *predominant use* of the house.

Strange rules

Stoves vs. hot plates

Steve's two-family property was located in a busy, downtown area teeming with single individuals. The property had a basement with a separate street entrance begging to be made into a studio apartment. Zoning would not allow the house to be converted into three "apartments."

Investigating further, Steve discovered that what constituted an "apartment" for zoning was a *rented area containing a stove*. The apartment could have a refrigerator, sink, and microwave. It could have an instant hot water tap, and it could have a hot plate. But no stove. Steve bought an inexpensive microwave, hot plate, and instant hot water tap and had no problem renting his uniquely equipped studio apartment.

If there is a moral to this story, it is to probe into the nuances of zoning objections.

"By three or more non-related people"

Zoning laws sometimes prohibit dwellings to be occupied by more than three non-related people. This assures that communes and other non-desirable groups won't mar the neighborhood's residential tranquility.

"Three or more non-related people" is a landlord's problem, especially when renting to more than three non-related students, non-married adults, or families with more than three non-related foster children.

Courts have been somewhat tolerant in granting "family" status to non-related individuals. Family status has been granted to groups of priests and other non-related clergy and to families caring for more than three foster children. The winning argument has been that the group functions as a "family."

The flip side has courts now and then enforcing "three or more non-related people" zoning rules. One disturbing case in my own state had a jurisdiction enforcing a "three or more non-related" rule requiring a foster family to evict several homeless, non-related children from their home. Everyone praised the foster parents, but rules were rules, which had to be enforced.

In-law apartments

You will sometimes see houses advertised with "in-law" apartments. "In-law" apartment has a cozy, family ring to it.

Be careful. Houses with in-law apartments often are not zoned for two families. No separate zoning exception exists, i.e., that a single-family house can be subdivided to accommodate members of the same family. Buyers must realize that "in-law" apartments are not separate apartments which can be separately rented. As with all rules, there are exceptions. Some housing codes allow a second living space within a home when the space is earmarked for a family member.

Excepted use is specific.

A corner store in a residential neighborhood may have a video store for which zoning variance was obtained through "excepted use." Don't assume you can later rent the store for a laundromat or grocery. The excepted use may be just for that particular excepted use (video store). Separate excepted use permission may have to be obtained to rent the premises as a grocery store, laundromat, etc.

Historic districts

Sometimes, new landlords get more than they bargained for when purchasing buildings in historic districts. Zoning laws dictate the types of windows, window treatments, doors, outdoor lights, fences, etc. that can be used. Maintaining rental houses in historic districts can sometimes get complicated.

Example: Historic district zoning might not allow air-conditioning units in street-facing windows. Where central air-conditioning is lacking, this may necessitate summer and winter bedrooms. Summer bedrooms are in the back of the house where window units *are* permitted, and winter bedrooms are in the front of the house which usually receives more sunlight.

Condominium and townhouse associations

Similar restrictions exist when purchasing a condominium apartment or townhouse. Today, three-quarters of the homes in suburban developments, especially planned communities, are under some sort of restrictive covenants. This affects what landlords and tenants can do with property.

Rules cover exterior improvements, fences, color of window drapes, lawn decorations, basketball backboards, clothes lines, mail boxes, house numbers, and outdoor lighting. Rules control whether the owner of a condominium unit is even allowed to lease a unit and to whom.

Are these rules enforceable?

Yes. Courts have sustained the rights of people among themselves to agree to all sorts of restrictions not contrary to public policy. These laws are generally upheld, but there are limits to such power, for example

— whether a condominium or townhouse association can fine offending members
— whether the association can remove private property from commonly owned areas
— whether the association can bar prospective occupants on racial or religious grounds
— whether the association can ban window displays of Christmas lights or other holiday decorations.

Restrictive covenants

"Restrictive covenants" is another term used when discussing planned communities. As do zoning laws, restrictive covenants dictate what owners can do with property. They differ from zoning laws in that they are *private contractual regulations*, not government enactments.

Example: Paul sells Mary a parcel of land recorded with the restriction that if the land is ever used for a shoe store, it reverts back to the original owner. If Mary or subsequent buyers construct a shoe store, Paul or his assigns can bring suit.

This, of course, is an extreme example. Some restrictive covenants have been held to be unenforceable as against public policy. Examples are restrictive covenants against selling or renting to members of religious or racial minority groups.

Property owners sometimes have to be creative to circumvent restrictive covenants.

Example: One community restricted satellite dishes but not outdoor picnic tables and umbrellas. One resourceful homeowner installed an outdoor picnic table with a satellite dish built into the picnic table umbrella. The community association was unsuccessful in their challenge.

This is a whole new area of law, but generally, restrictive covenants must be consistent with state and federal constitutional rights.

Zoning appeals

If you plan to expand, subdivide, or obtain a variance, you may have to go before a Zoning Appeals Board. Where stakes are high, counsel may be in order. But as owner of your property, you are in a good position to represent yourself.

Caution: The axiom among lawyers is: "A lawyer with himself as lawyer, has a fool for an attorney." That said, if you do your homework and have successfully represented yourself at traffic court, you should be able to handle a zoning appeal.

Prior to the hearing

Before the hearing, you must submit plats and diagrams of your plans. Plats and diagrams have to be on certain types and size of paper and must conform to certain court rules. Unless you are an architect, artist, or have done this before, ask the court clerk for names of people who prepare diagrams and plats.

The local community also needs notice of your plans. Some jurisdictions require publication in area newspapers (again, certain requirements must be followed), and/or some require notice of the proposed action and court date posted on the property. Again, certain rules must be followed, i.e., wording, sign size, letter size, where posted on building, length of time posted, etc. The zoning office may even be able to recommend a sign-maker familiar with the court's sign requirements.

> *Note*: Make sure your zoning sign remains posted. It is not an excuse that someone removed the sign. In my community, the zoning board sends a photographer to the property to assure that the zoning notice was properly posted.

The zoning hearing

The local zoning office will schedule a hearing date for you. From the time the sign is up until the time of the hearing, there is homework for you.

Try to find out what kind of opposition is lined up against you. If opposition is minimal or none, you do not want to come before the board with overkill. However, if substantial opposition is expected, there is no such thing as overkill.

> *Example*: At a zoning hearing for a corner bar wanting to expand in an historic area of my city, *each side* brought over twenty witnesses to testify. It was neighbor vs. neighbor, politician vs. politician, neighborhood preservation group vs. neighborhood preservation group.

Try to obtain supporting letters from local politicians and neighborhood groups. If this is not possible, try to get letters from politicians or neighborhood groups saying that they have no position one way or the other concerning your request. Sometimes, a neutral position from parties who normally protest is construed as tacit support.

If you believe your request is in the public interest, get clergy support.

Example: While community groups may oppose group homes or subdivided houses, opposition may be muffled by clergy support.

Needs vs. wants

Develop strategy demonstrating need, not merely wants. If for example, you seek a variance for an outdoor deck on a rental unit, concentrate on need. You *need* that deck to attract decent tenants. You *need* that deck to preserve neighborhood housing values. You *need* that deck to compete with houses in the suburbs.

Self-representation requirements

—*Clean appearance.* You don't need a $600 designer suit but greasy overalls turn some people off.

—*Regard for protocol.* For the time you are before the board you must treat the board with respect and follow their procedural rules.

—*Self-control.* You must hold your cool against witnesses testifying against you. Stick to the facts. Calmly answer board members' questions.

—*Some homework.* You must become familiar with your case. Besides *your* personal gain, what will the *community* gain?

Winning may be two-sided.

Often, a zoning win is conditional. Yes, the ruling reads, you may increase the number of rental units or may add an addition, but

— you must increase the number of parking spaces

— you must bring the entire house wiring, plumbing, etc. up to the new codes

— you must include one low-income apartment.

Note: At the hearing, you may wish to use some of these points as bargaining chips. Volunteer to do that which you might have done anyway.

The Achilles heel of zoning

Zoning is defeated in four instances:

— where there is too much ambiguity. Zoning laws stating that houses must be of the "same architectural style or design" have been voided as being too vague. Ordinances should be specific, and "interpretation should not be left to the whims and caprice of administrative agencies."
— where zoning is used to promote segregation or exclude certain disadvantaged groups. This occurs most often in areas requiring building lots to be multi-acred, thereby precluding disadvantaged groups.
— where it is confiscatory. All zoning involves some degree of confiscation, but where confiscation is unreasonable, zoning ordinances fail. Zoning must relate to the legitimate objectives of police powers, that is, government's right to regulate land use to protect the health, morals, and welfare of its citizens.
— where laws change. Zoning laws are not set in stone. Needs and circumstances change. Rather than just complain, landlords are beginning to take the helm at changing zoning laws.

CHAPTER 14

SELLING PROPERTY PROFITABLY
DURING GOOD TIMES AND BAD

In this chapter, your hat as seller is different from that worn in Chapter two as buyer. Different strategy is involved.

Part I
Selling During Good Times

Timing
The climax of property ownership is selling at a profit and to good owners. Timing is crucial. The time to sell is when you *want* to, not when you *have* to.

The time to sell is when:
— all major house components work well: heat, air conditioner, roof, etc. If one of these components is broken, fix it. Prospective buyers are scared of repair and replacement costs and deduct more than they should from their offering price.
— the house is occupied by decent tenants. Prospective buyers are afraid of empty houses because they never know how long it will take to rent or the expenses needed to make a house rentable.
— the house is not run-down. While needed repairs may only be cosmetic, they drive the house price down far in excess of their cost.
— you, the landlord, are in good health and not in the midst of a personal or physical crisis. Buyers use seller's infirmary to their advantage, as indeed they should.
— you are not in the midst of a divorce. I know a case where seller

purposely accepted low offers so that his spouse would receive less money!

— long before you move. Leverage is lost when buyer knows that you are being transferred out of state and have to sell, or that you are retiring and relocating to a new home in Florida.

— you are not in a financial bind. You will never receive your asking price if you're perceived to be in financial straits.

— a major improvement is announced for the area. The best time here is during construction. Hopes are highest at this point. After construction is finished, things generally revert to where they were before.

Note: Don't underestimate the ripple effect of new construction in the area. Franchisers such as McDonald's extensively research an area before opening a new location. That is why so few of their stores fail. Banks also require independent research to confirm an area's potential before lending money for large projects. As a rule of thumb, you can safely follow McDonald's.

— your accountant or tax advisor recommends it. Perhaps you have used all your depreciation. Perhaps you should defer the sale until next year. Too often, sales are made without tax consideration. Large profit makes little sense if it has to be turned over to the tax collector.

— the economy is good. You don't want to sell during times of national disaster or when financial analysts predict rough times ahead.

— no one else on the block is selling. Excess houses for sale drives prices down. Nothing scares prospective buyers more than seeing several *"For Sale"* signs on a block.

Seasons are important.

Not without reason, experts advise listing houses during spring or summer. Similar logic applies to investment property.

—There are extra daylight hours to show the property.

—Trees and gardens are in bloom; people are in streets.

Fall buyers always wonder about utility bills and how the heating system or roof will hold out during the coming winter. Fall buyers deduct more than they should from their offering price. If you must sell in the fall, and the house has a working fireplace, light a fire. It conjures up feelings of warmth, stimulates conversation, and highlights a major property asset.

Winter is a good time to sell if your house has a small backyard or poor landscaping. While buyers make a point of walking around a property during other times of the year, they often by-pass walking around the property when the ground is wet, frozen, or snow-covered.

Do you need a real estate agent?
Advantages
—Agents draw buyers from a larger area and network with other agents to bring serious buyers to the property.
—Agents are objective and help you set a realistic price to get the property sold.
—Agents show property on their time, not yours.
—Agents work on commission and have a special incentive to get the highest price.

Example 1: No real estate agent: Seller asks $80,000, buyer offers $60,000. After prolonged negotiation compromise is reached at $70,000.

Example 2: Agent: Seller asks $80,000, buyer wishes to offer $60,000. Agent tells buyer not to waste everyone's time and convinces buyer to offer $70,000. After prolonged negotiation, compromise is reached at $75,000! (While agents must present all legitimate offers, in real life, agents discourage buyers from submitting excessively low offers.)

—Agents can plead ignorance to certain probing questions about your property and say that they don't know. If you the owner lie, you can be legally liable for misrepresentation.

Note: Scores of lawsuits are filed each year against *agents* for misrepresenting or failing to disclose defects that they knew or should have known. Agents are becoming more careful.

—Agents have expertise handling questions involving sales contracts, inspections, appraisals, financing, closings, *etc.*

—Agents act as middlemen and arbitrators and sometimes play Solomon to get buyers and sellers to agree on price and terms.

—While trying to act as middleman, the agent legally works for you, the seller, because you pay the commission.

Disadvantages
(Most disadvantages can be remedied by a prior understanding or special arrangement with the agent.)

—The agent charges a hefty 5 to 7 percent commission for finding a buyer. Commission is negotiable, especially if property is expected to sell quickly or at a good price. The opposite is true too. Negotiation is limited if a house is expected to take longer to sell. You may even be asked to pay a premium!

—Agents are not only trying to sell your house but also other houses. Agents try to sell houses where they get the most commission. (For those trying to sell a house quickly, many recommend offering agents a bonus in addition to their regular commission.)

—While the agent is supposed to work for you, the seller, because you pay the commission, sometimes you get the impression the agent is really working for the buyer and is asking *you* to make unfair concessions to conclude the sale.

—Agents get preoccupied with their personal affairs; they may be moving, preparing for company, or in the midst of their own major or minor crisis. Try to secure agents who work in teams. It is like getting two agents for the price of one.

—For the commission agents receive, you may be able to secure a buyer cheaper with your own advertising and having someone else show the property.

Note: A misconception persists that if property is listed, no commission is due to the agent if *seller* finds a buyer. Where agents are given *exclusive rights to sell*, court cases go in the *agent's* favor. Again, this is a negotiable item.

—Sometimes, agents have their own biases as to whom they will show the house. Some bias is against the law, especially where it pertains to age, sex, race, religion, nation origin, or handicap. But agent bias can also include non-protected areas that nonetheless hinder the sale of your house, i.e., agents who chose not to show houses to people driving sports cars, pick-up trucks, etc.

—For the commission agents receive, you can sometimes cosmetically improve the property to give it necessary curb appeal. A $50,000 house sold at a 7 percent commission gives an agent $3,500. This is money that can be otherwise used to upgrade the house to "cream puff" condition.

Which agent to use?

It's tempting to use your wife's cousin or your neighbor's friend as listing agent. After all, the reasoning goes, all agents have access to multiple listings. Why shouldn't a relative or friend participate in the commission? But is this best for you?

Agents who are close relatives or friends sometimes offer to "kick-back" part of their commission. Besides being illegal in most areas, this ultimately may not be in your best interest.

Just as you didn't buy the house without shopping around, so too must you carefully select your agent.

You want an agent who:
— is accessible and who returns calls. After taking your listing, many agents disappear and refuse to answer phone calls.
— is hungry for business. Many agents are part-timers, retirees, housewives, etc. who don't like showing houses nights, week ends, or when children are home or off from school.
— lives in the neighborhood where the house is being sold. Agents who live in the neighborhood have a vested interest in seeing that good people purchase the property.
— has an existing list of prospective candidates. These agents are active in church, PTA, neighborhood improvement associations, etc.
— has an existing relationship with financial institutions. These agents give lenders business in good times and in bad and are also familiar with alternative forms of financing.
— is the best salesperson in the office, not necessarily the person with the most listings. You can ask for this information; it is not confidential.

— can give you references. Prior clients are top candidates for suggestions and tips.

How property is listed
Properties are listed in one of three ways: open listing, exclusive right to sell, and exclusive agency.

Open listing
Property is listed with an agent, but the owner can list his property with any number of agents. Commission goes to the agent who actually sells the property. The owner can sell the property himself without paying anyone a commission.

Exclusive right to sell
Under this form, the agent gets his commission when property is sold by anyone, even if the owner secured the sale.

Don't expect the broker to even tell you about the clause buried in the contract. It reads: "The undersigned owner agrees to pay Broker a commission . . . if said property is sold or exchanged directly *by the owner* or through Broker . . . (emphasis added).

Numerous cases have gone to court over this form. Be wary.

Exclusive agency
Exclusive agency is the recommended form of listing. Under this form, if owner sells the property himself, he does not pay anyone commission. The owner though is precluded from listing the property with another agent.

Don't expect the broker to volunteer the exclusive agency form which lets the owner sell the property without paying commission.

> *Note:* Some agents ask for a period of time, i.e., seventy-two hours, before placing the property on multiple list. This gives the agent a short period of time to exclusively show the property to the private customers and hopefully earn the entire commission.

Sale by owner
You need a certain temperament to sell your house. You will have situations starting off on the wrong foot because prospective buyers

came late or came with small children. Some prospective buyers demean and critique every part of the house to justify the lower price they offer. As owner, you are more apt to lose your cool.

Most people simply do not have the time, experience, or temperament to handle owner-sales. Look in the classified section of your newspaper. There is a reason why most houses are listed by agents and not owners.

Brokers and agents protected

A cross between an owner's sale and an agent's sale is an owner advertising property with a notation stating, "Brokers and agents protected." Here, the owner recognizes that an agent may find a prospective buyer. The owner and agent negotiate a separate fee which is usually lower than if the agent solely handled the sale.

"For Sale" Signs

Unless your property is in a neighborhood where "For Sale" signs bring immediate results, signs attached to buildings are not recommended.

On vacant houses, this is especially true. "For Sale" signs highlight the fact that the house is unoccupied and invite vandals to visit. Contrary to popular belief, many insurance policies do not cover damage cause by vandalism, and some have other exclusions if the house is vacant for more than thirty days. In today's market, you can expect a house to be vacant more than thirty days.

"For Sale" signs do not rest well with existing tenants. Would you like to be a tenant with a "House For Sale" sign in your window, or on your lawn? It is one thing if tenants know a house is on the market. It is another where a sign constantly reminds them that they will soon have new owners.

Unless you live in a neighborhood where "For Sale" signs bring instant results, such signs blatantly advertise that you can't otherwise privately sell your property. The longer a sign sits on your property, the bigger price reduction buyers expect.

With a "For Sale" sign, you have to answer every curiosity-seeker seeing the sign. It's not uncommon for nosy neighbors to ask to see the house. However, don't shoo these people away. Even though they are not serious candidates for your house, the fact remains that they live in the neighborhood and are in the best position to recommend your house to others.

Testing the market

Private sellers, and sometimes even real estate agents, test the market by initially offering the house at the highest imaginable price in the hopes that some unknowledgeable person takes it.

Sometimes this works. You may have a buyer who wants the particular house or location no matter the cost. You may have buyers coming from high-priced areas, and your property is a steal. You may have buyers who are not paying for the house, rather a company is paying, or there are generous in-laws, or buyers are independently wealthy and don't care about price.

Testing the market works when time is not of the essence, and you can afford to wait it out or offer it later at a reduced price. If your house is vacant, that is not the time to test the market. Besides exposing your house to vandalism, during vacant months you have other expenses, i.e., taxes, insurance, depreciation, interest, cost of capital, etc.

More often than not, testing the market works against you. Your house is listed at an excessive price, and there are not even any nibbles. This is especially true in a buyer's market where many houses are up for sale. While some buyers actually enjoy bargaining down high-priced houses, most buyers shy away from heavy bargaining and prefer to deal with realistically priced houses.

If your house doesn't sell in a reasonable amount of time, people assume there are other things wrong with the house. This brings down the property value even more. When people see you drastically reducing price, they think they can get you to go down even more.

When a house doesn't immediately sell, your agent begins to lose interest as well and is usually preoccupied with more current listings.

The other way people "test the market" is by first trying to sell the house themselves. When that doesn't work, the private "For Sale" signs come down, and colorful listing agent signs go up. While you can't blame owners for trying to sell property themselves, to the man on the street, a change of signs is an open proclamation that the house did not sell the first time, and either there is something wrong with the house or the owner is now prepared to take less.

The irony of the later scenario is that the owner is not willing to take less. In fact he now asks *more*. When the owner replaces the private "For Sale" sign with an agent's sign, the owner must raise the price to now cover the agent's commission. If before the owner asked $100,000, he now needs $107,000 to cover the agent's 7 percent commission.

Setting price

Every seller for "phase one" is allowed to test the market to see if property sells for the quixotic dream price. As noted above, even unrealistic sellers sometimes get lucky.

"Phase two" requires the seller to seriously set a price. Think of what you would offer for the house if *you* were the buyer.

Some sellers purposely inflate the price 20 to 30 percent for negotiation. Some sellers even label the price "asking price," as if to say, the price isn't real, make an offer.

Some sellers signal that *limited* negotiation is acceptable. They do this by advertising a property at $69,900. Most buyers, even those who don't usually dicker, will ask that the $900 be stricken to make it an even $69,000. More aggressive buyers will assume that $69,900 means an even $65,000.

Sellers wanting to keep firm prices are advised to set prices in firm, even amounts—$65,000, $70,000. This is a signal to buyers that seller has shaved off all fat. Some sellers even put this in their advertising, i.e. "$85,000, firm." Pugnacious buyers will still haggle, but it does discourage many from trying.

Escape clauses

Be wary of "escape clauses" shrewd buyers insert for a way out of the contract. While unfortunately this is part of the negotiation process, you are not obligated to grant these concessions. Some sample escape clauses:

—*Attorney review clause.* This clause lets buyer sign the contract conditioned upon his attorney okaying the contract. If buyer finds a better house, the attorney finds something objectionable. Your attorney, of course, can challenge buyer's attorney's good faith, but this can be expensive.

—*Inspection and financing clauses.* As seller you have a limited choice on these two options. Few buyers are prepared to offer a cash contract for a property in its "as is" condition or without a financing condition. The best you can do is to put a time limit on these clauses.

—*House appraisal clause.* This clause is used where buyer needs the property appraised at a certain value to secure a loan.

Buyers use all sorts of imaginative devices to escape. They get inspectors to come up with the most picky points. They will go back to the bank with negative information about themselves to cause the bank to withdraw a previously approved loan commitment. Again, your attorney can challenge buyer's good faith, but this is time-consuming and expensive.

> *Note*: Sometimes it is *seller* who has to insert an "escape clause" into the contract, particularly a clause saying, "subject to the existing tenant's right of first refusal." Some tenants have demanded that this clause be inserted in the lease. In some areas, it is the local law. In such cases tenants must be offered the house at the same price and at the same terms as the potential buyer.

Inspection reports

Unless you have an "as is" contract, you must be on guard for buyer's inspector whose job is to find things wrong with the property. Some buyers have second thoughts about the property and use inspectors as deal-breakers. In theory, the seller can challenge the buyer's report by having his own inspector rebut the first inspector's report. This is costly and should be done only if great sums of money are involved.

Most inspection reports are not used as deal-breakers. They're just picky nuisances. Some sellers wisely take this into account when negotiating the price. They include a little reserve to pay for minor improvements called for by the inspection report.

> *Note*: Especially expect "inspection repair requests" where there is seller's listing agent and buyer's real estate agent. In these situations, even though seller pays both agents' commissions, the listing agent becomes seller's advocate while buyer's agent assumes buyer's cause.

Must seller make repairs?

Some sellers mistakenly believe they must make every repair noted in the inspector's report. That is not so. A seller does not have to do anything! An inspector's report is only supposed to give buyer insight to the property condition, and where there is a "subject to a satisfactory inspection report" contingency, an "out" if required repairs are significant.

The key word here is "significant," and many battles have been fought over this word.

As seller, don't be intimidated by buyer's unreasonable demands. An old house that you are selling is precisely that. Doors squeak, tiles are missing, and there are cracks in the walls. If the twenty-year old roof needs to be replaced, that is what buyers should expect from a twenty-year-old roof. *Sellers often do better by holding firm.* This is the house, take it or leave it.

Consider buyer's psyche. The buyer has already made a mental decision to purchase the property. The buyer has time invested in this property. He has put energy into negotiating a price with the seller. He has given a check in earnest money and laid out money for an inspector. Deep down, he does not want this time and money wasted. The buyer's fallback position is to take the house anyway. But this being a free country, he's allowed to *ask* hoping that a nervous seller will accede to his request.

Wear-the-seller-down technique

Be on guard against buyers who use the *wear-the-seller-down technique.* Such buyers get the most out of sellers at the contract writing stage. Then, when seller thinks he has given all that can be given, buyer exacts more at the inspection level. And then, when seller thinks he has given every last concession, buyer exacts more at the financing approval level. Finally, after seller gives in on all these areas, buyer squeezes one bit more at the pre-closing level.

Prematurely putting property up for sale

This is akin to testing the waters. You can understand why sellers sometimes fall prey to putting property up for sale when it is cluttered or bad tenants still occupy the house. In a seller's market, sellers sometimes succeed. But more often than not, prematurely offering property for sale works against the seller.

Puffing

Certain exaggeration is permitted. You can call your house, charming, exquisite, cream puff, or any other adjective subject to a point of view.

Misrepresentation

There is a legal difference between misrepresenting and failing to inform.

Misrepresentation can be by *word*, i.e., stating your house is twenty years old, when it is really thirty years old; that your house has 150-amp house power when it really has 100-amp power.

Misrepresentation can be by *deed*, i.e. covering water-damaged basement walls with paneling. As you can imagine, when this occurs, aggrieved buyers have several recourses.

Aggrieved buyers can elect to void the contract, especially if the misrepresentation is "material." If the house was represented as having gas heat and it had oil heat, that may be material. If the house was represented as twenty years old, and it was really twenty-one years old, the misrepresentation probably isn't material and it may be difficult to void the contract.

Aggrieved buyers can hold you to the difference, i.e. the cost to upgrade 100-amp service to the promised 150-amp service.

Aggrieved buyers can ignore the misrepresentation. This is what usually happens. If sellers are otherwise decent and the house price is otherwise fair, buyers find other reasons to take the house at the agreed price.

At one time, there was less of a duty for sellers to inform buyers of defects. The rule of *caveat emptor*—"buyer beware," applied, and in most jurisdictions, it *still* applies. It was felt that buyers can have the house checked by their own inspectors and appraisers.

Over the years, this legal principle has eroded, and whether fair or not, some jurisdictions now require sellers to disclose *known defects*, especially where not readily evident. You may have to inform buyers that the house once had water damage or termites. You may be under an obligation to inform buyers that the major tenant has indicated an intention to move. Some jurisdictions are considering requiring agents to preliminarily investigate the property's condition.

Experts recommend that sellers honestly represent the condition of the house. As a rule, buyers will usually accept defects in a house if seller is up-front about it. No one likes surprises.

Give them more, not less.

A good sales rule to follow whether renting or selling is to entice the renter, or buyer, by constantly offering more. Your initial advertisement has some, or many of the house's good features, but not all.

At the next contact level, usually phone inquiry, more favorable information is given.

Finally, when the buyer or renter actually appears at the property, even more good news is given. If you want, save one last piece of good news to clinch the deal or to assure buyer or renter that he did well.

The flip side is a situation that advertises a house or apartment with three bedrooms and a fenced-yard when in actuality one bedroom is in the basement, and the yard's fence is falling apart. Buyer expecting a three-bedroom, fenced yard house is not going to accept less.

Showing the house

Showing a house to potential buyers involves many of the same techniques discussed in the rental section. However, since stakes are higher on a sale, extra effort on your part is required.

Transportation

There are several reasons why you should pick up the prospective buyer at his house and not just have the buyer meet you at the property and then leave after seeing the property.

—By picking up buyer at his house, you literally have more insight as to "where buyer is coming from." You have more things now to talk about.

—You know from the start that buyer will show. Too often, sellers are kept waiting at the property. (Some buyers purposely use this strategy to weaken sellers.)

—You get a chance to prepare buyer in advance for flaws and deficiencies. Where there are flaws, *exaggerate* the flaws. Buyers will be relieved to find the property's faults hardly problems at all. Minimize the property's assets—the buyer will be pleasantly surprised when he sees that the small bedrooms are really not so small after all.

—As driver, you select the prettiest way to the property. You don't want the buyer going down the wrong blocks or being turned off before getting to the property.

—As driver, you sit in the control seat. Your opinion has more authority. The buyer, being transported, has a certain indebtedness to you.

—As driver, you control the length of the visit and get an additional

chance in the car to answer questions or relieve anxieties.
—When you stop to let the buyer out, buyer may wish to invite you
into his house. This gives you an extra chance to get to know each
other better, hash out disagreements, and make the sale.

Note: If you plan to transport more than one buyer, it helps if
your car is a four-door model. It is terrible to start a relationship with potential buyers struggling to get in and out of a car.
Too, you are now acting as a salesman; get rid of excess car
junk and other non-professional items.

Part II
Selling During Bad Times

What if your house just won't sell?
Secure an objective opinion. Let's say a major reason your house
isn't selling is because it has an old oil furnace. Buyers are either scared
of high fuel bills or that the furnace will have to be replaced.

To facilitate the sale you can:
— offer 500 gallons of oil to fill buyer's tank for the winter.
— offer to pay buyer's oil furnace repair contract for the next two
years. Repair contracts are in the $75 to $100 range and assure
buyers that the furnace will be maintained.
— offer to pay $1,000 (or other figure) toward oil furnace
replacement or conversion to another system.

Independent appraisal. If your asking price is perceived to be too
high, pay for an independent appraisal showing the house to be worth
your asking price, and maybe even more. It is a good selling tactic to
sell the house below the appraised value. This reassures buyers they
not only got a good deal, they got a *great* deal.

Old appliances. If objective analysis says the house won't sell because
appliances are old and buyers are scared of replacement/repair costs,
offer a home warranty guaranteeing all major systems for a certain
period after the sale. This is a $150 to $300 option many real estate

agents offer sellers.

If the house is messy, offer buyer a year's worth of maid service. If the house is in a bad school district, offer $1,000 (or whatever figure it takes) for buyer's child's private schooling. If there are no children in the neighborhood, offer a free year's membership to the local community center or pool. Buyers appreciate seller honesty. Here, in a dignified way, you recognize the house's liabilities and offer to remedy the situation the best way possible.

Vacant house. Vacant houses are foreboding. Your job as seller is to make property less foreboding. At minimum, put light bulbs back in the sockets, toilet paper in the bathrooms, and paper towels in the kitchen. Bare windows should at least have window shades.

Turning heat and water off

I don't know why landlords shut off heat and water in vacant houses, but it is totally wrong. There is not a buyer in this country who doesn't instinctively try turning on water in a bathroom or kitchen sink to test the water pressure. Even if they know nothing about how a furnace functions, buyers want assurance that it works.

There is nothing more embarrassing when showing a house than having to use the bathroom yourself or having to deny bathroom facilities to a potential buyer because water was turned off.

In the winter, landlords may fear pipes freezing and bursting during a cold spell. But even in cold snaps, experts advise not shutting water off, rather letting a trickle flow in a basement or lower-floor sink.

> *Note*: In areas where tenants direct water utility companies to shut water off, tenants when asked by landlords will sometimes leave water on for a short period to allow landlords to fix and rent the place. Landlords might want to consider requiring this in the lease, or throw in a sweetener. Where this fails, landlords should really consider turning the water on themselves and deem it part of the price of selling a property.

Toilets

Even if the water is on, don't ignore the toilets in a vacant house. Toilets in vacant houses quickly develop rust stains around the water edge. Besides being unsightly, stains and dirt are dead giveaways that the house has been vacant for a long period of time. This can negatively effect your selling price. Keep an inexpensive brush beside the toilet and swish it around every now and then. Also, keep an air freshener in the room.

Turning utilities off

Landlords have a reputation of being some of the cheapest people in the world. Every reader of this book has been shown at least one piece of real estate property where power has been turned off. You wouldn't think of going into an automobile showroom to look at cars with showroom lights off; why should houses be different?

We know why landlords do this; we're basically a frugal lot. We got to this position in life precisely because we are not spend-thrifts.

It's not that landlords turn power off. No landlord does that. It's just that after a tenant leaves and turns the power off, the landlord does nothing to restore power in the landlord's name so that he can either rent the house or apartment or sell it.

With the power on, landlords have the additional option of showing the property at night, after work. With power on, buyers are reassured that the systems work, and the landlord can show other parts of the house without having to use a flashlight.

> *Note*: In some areas, the gas and electric company allows landlords to automatically assume utility service. Deposits and applications are waived. Check with your utility company if this can be arranged.

If these sales attempts at rectifying a bad situation do not work, be prepared to initiate the following two phases.

Phase I. Make sure you've exhausted the obvious:
—You made all the necessary cosmetic improvements that you're going to make.
—Your asking price is reasonable and can be substantiated by an independent appraisal.
—You offered to pay buyer's points, title insurance, and whatever else is necessary to close the deal.
—You offered owner-financing.
—You offered a bonus to agents.

—You offered rent with an option to buy.
—You offered to pay buyer's moving expenses.
—You offered to pay buyer's closing costs.

Owner-financing

Just because you agreed to owner-finance all or part of the sales price does not mean caution can be ignored. Get help from a mortgage broker (they're listed in the Yellow Pages). For a fee, approximately $250, mortgage brokers secure credit reports, references, and employment history. Some sellers get buyers to assume this fee.

Mortgage brokers also assure that the deal is properly structured. Properly structured mortgages have a certain resale value, i.e., people buy and sell mortgages. Since as lender you are in effect "the bank," you can require the same safeguards banks require, i.e., escrow accounts for insurance and taxes. Where a second mortgage is involved, you can require the first mortgagee (i.e., the bank) to notify you of buyer's default.

These cautionary notes are not meant to scare you from owner-financing. Many sellers owner-finance with favorable results. They continue a relationship with their former house and get a higher rate of return than they could get depositing the sales proceeds in a bank.

> *Note*: If during any single year you sell more than two properties via owner-financing, you may wish to consult a lawyer (I'm sorry). Some states label you a mortgage banker or broker (honest), even if you finance your own property! You may need additional licensing.

Phase II. If your investment property still has not sold, you are ready for the next phase which employs auto-dealer tactics:

— gifts to people who *look at the house*

> *Note*: Consider also an open house for real estate *agents*. They can be enticed to view the property with food, i.e., lunch, pen and pencil sets, etc.

— gifts of television sets, microwaves, VCRs, washer/dryer, vacations, furniture, etc. to people making *bona fide offers*
— promises of gifts to people *who actually buy*, i.e., outdoor swing

set, patio furniture, house alarm system.

Continuing with auto-dealer tactics, you advertise catchy lines such as:
— selling below appraised value
— owner transferred, must sell
— no reasonable offer refused

and one of my favorites:
— PLEASE! PLEASE! Do not buy elsewhere until you have seen this incredible home.

Creative financing

Financing is buyer's responsibility, but when your house doesn't sell, financing becomes *your* challenge.

Get your real estate agent to share your burden.

Example: Seller's property lists for $100,000; buyer wants 95 percent owner-financing. Seller hesitates to accept the offer since, besides seller's closing costs, seller also has to pay a 7 percent real estate commission, i.e., $7,000. For this *sale*, the owner might have to come up with several thousand dollars. One remedy is for the seller to ask the agent to accept the commission in installments. The agent is assured of the sale and the owner does not have to immediately come up with $7,000.

Marketing a package: Making one plus one equal three

Sometimes it pays to work with neighbors to get a better collective deal than each neighbor can get individually.

Example: Your fairly run-down $60,000 rental property in a busy or expensive neighborhood adjoins other $60,000 fairly run-down properties. Instead of listing your house for $60,000, you *and your neighbors* list your properties as a package. A pre-assembled package is a developer's dream and is worth extra money to a developer.

Land installment contracts

In some areas, these are known as *contracts for deed*. Under either name, ownership remains with seller until buyer finishes his payment obligation. In these situations, seller continues to have *legal* title and buyer has *equitable* title.

The advantage to seller and buyer is that settlement fees are kept to a bare minimum since they are deferred. Because title ownership does not change, there are no costly title searches, transfer taxes, recording fees, etc. (If you are ever in the position of buyer, it may be advisable for you to order a title and credit report.)

Another advantage to a land installment contract is that, if buyer intends to shortly sell the property, title may pass from the original owner to the newest buyer bypassing the interim buyer.

While title remains with the seller who has more protection than merely holding a mortgage, two caveats are in order:

—Because title rests with seller, seller is responsible for building violations and liabilities arising from the property.

—If buyer does not fulfill his contract obligations, expensive foreclosure procedures may still be required.

Auctions

Auctions used to be the sales technique of last resort. Of late, auctions have become an increasingly popular way of selling property. Make sure the auctioneer you select specializes in real estate. Such auctioneers arrange for proper publicity and sometimes maintain their own mailing lists of potential buyers.

> *Note:* Advance mailing to potential buyers can generate *absentee bidders*. These bidders do not attend the auction, but tender their bids to the auctioneer prior to the auction.

Sellers can elect to have either an *absolute auction* where the sale goes to the highest bid, or a *reserve auction* where seller reserves the right to accept or reject the highest bid.

Sellers pay fewer closing costs.

> *Example:* If the sales contract on a "regular" sale is signed January 1 and closing is February 15, seller pays real estate taxes until the date of closing. At an auction sale held January 1, buyer pays taxes *as of January 1*, even though buyer does not take possession until settlement.

Where buyer and seller traditionally split certain closing transfer costs (recording taxes, stamps), buyers at auction sales usually incur this expense.

Auctioneers' fees vary. Some charge an initial administrative fee plus receive a commission on the selling price, i.e., 6 percent. Some auctioneers also charge buyers a small percentage, i.e., percent.

Sellers can lower their auction costs by requiring a *buyer's premium*. This is a surcharge, typically 10 percent added to the successful bidding price to help pay for the auctioneer's administrative costs.

Where rental property is vacant, buyers are sometimes allowed to view the inside prior to the auction. This is known as an *exhibition preview*. Savvy buyers bring tape measures and their own knowledgeable engineering authorities.

> *Note*: Sellers sometimes are faced with situations where existing tenants refuse to allow the auctioned house to be viewed. The house will either have to be auctioned without an exhibition preview, or sellers will have to seek legal recourse. (Dale Carnegie students can think of other ways to get tenants to let them in.)

Auctions are absolute sales without contingency clauses. Property is purchased "as is," and buyer is obligated to appear at closing with cash or a certified check.

> *Note*: "As is" sales do not free seller from having to provide clear title. But clear title is just that. Seller does not guaranty that the house will be vacant.

Auction price, also called hammer price

In theory, auctioned property should sell for less because buyers assume more risk. However, auctions come with an added dimension, *hype of the crowd*. Houses at auction sell above value when the crowd is roused, and below market value when there is little enthusiasm.

> *Note*: Consider "multi-seller auctions," where auctioneers sell a group of houses belonging to different sellers. There are economics of advertising and marketing, and larger crowds are drawn. These auctions are often held in plush hotels with refreshments served.

When all else fails
   —*Charity raffle*. Donate the property to a charity raffle. Split proceeds with the charity, i.e., 50/50, 40/60, 90/10, etc.

Example: Tom's $50,000 house will not sell, and Tom tried every imaginable device. Tom donates the house to a charity raffle which assigns a $75,000 value to the house. The charity collects $75,000 in raffle receipts. At a 50/50 split, the charity pays Tom $37,500 and keeps $37,500 for its raffle efforts. Tom sells the house at only a $12,500 loss and may also realize an additional benefit, i.e., either a tax savings on his donation or a legitimate tax loss.

INDEX